ELIE WIESEL

A Voice for Humanity

D0830165

Elie Wiesel

ELIE WIESEL

A Voice for Humanity

Ellen Norman Stern

THE JEWISH PUBLICATION SOCIETY

Philadelphia and Jerusalem 5756 / 1996

Manufactured in the United States of America

Library of Congress Cataloguing-in-Publication Data

Stern, Ellen Norman.
Elie Wiesel: a voice for humanity / Ellen Norman Stern.
p. cm. — (JPS young biography series)
Includes bibliographical references and index.
ISBN 0-8276-0574-9 (cloth) — ISBN 0-8276-0616-8 (paper)
1. Wiesel, Elie, 1928– —Biography—Juvenile literature.
2. Authors, French—20th century—Biography—Juvenile literature.
3. Jewish authors—Biography—Juvenile literature.
4. Holocaust survivors—Biography—Juvenile literature. I. Title.
PQ2683. I32Z879 1996   95-49727
813' .54—dc20   CIP
[B]   AC

The following chapter titles were adapted from the titles of works
by Elie Wiesel:

The Face in the Window
An Interview Unlike Any Other
A Pilgrimage to the Past
The Jews of Silence
One Generation After
Memory May Be Our Only Answer

*For graciously granting permission to use photographs in
this book, the author wishes to thank Elie Wiesel and
Elirion, Inc.; William Coupon and Watusi, Inc.; Harold
Becker Productions, Inc.; Boston University Photo
Service; and Culver Pictures.*

Cover and frontispiece photos
courtesy of William Coupon.
Designed and typeset by Book Design Studio II

For
Lauren, Alex, and Rachel
with blessings

CONTENTS

CONTENTS

ACKNOWLEDGMENTS

Not long ago I was between trains in the waiting room
of a German railroad station when I overheard three
women in conversation. Not all their words were
audible to me, but several times I heard them use the
term "foreigner" and "stay behind their own borders,"
accompanied by facial expressions that left no doubt
of the women's feelings of dislike.

I was troubled by what I heard. Whether these were
references to Turkish "guest workers" or reunited East
Germans I did not know, but the tone of the remarks
brought back unpleasant memories of my childhood
in a similar setting, a time when such comments were
aimed at Jewish people.

Then I thought: What would Elie Wiesel do at this
moment? How would he react to such a scene? Once
more it became clear to me how the words of Elie

Wiesel, whether in writing or speech, have become important to a whole generation. And how amazing it is that the work of one person who survived a journey into hell could influence so many.

Elie Wiesel has spent his life chronicling his experiences and warning the world not to forget what happens when intolerance and violence take over. He has become a symbol of peace whose lessons of caring and concern must live on. Those lessons may save future generations from destruction.

Mr. Wiesel has remained a friend since my first interview with him a long time ago. I am deeply grateful to him for his interest and good wishes. Some of the photographs used in this book were graciously lent to me by him and I thank Martha Hauptman and Renée Spitz, his assistants, for making them available. It is important at this point to mention that this book claims in no way to be an authorized biography, but is an attempt to introduce the young reader to the life and times of a "great man in Israel."

This is my second chance to write about Elie Wiesel, and I am glad to be able to bring his story up to date. I owe this chance to my friend Janice L. Booker, who knows how important it is to me to pass on this particular story to those who come after us. Janice introduced my work to Bruce J. Black of the Jewish Publication Society, who encouraged me to write a second book about Elie Wiesel and became its editor. His guidance and friendship have made the writing process a delight for me.

I thank Larry and Marlyn, Michael and Amy for

their understanding and patience with me. To my husband Harold goes a special debt of gratitude for seeing me through yet another book. Without my family it would not have happened.

ENS

ELIE WIESEL

A Voice for Humanity

1

The Prophecy

They waited a long time that autumn morning in 1936. Through the room's small window the tops of the distant Carpathian Mountains were visible. Bathed in weak sunlight the mountain range circled their town of Sighet in Transylvania. Dozens of pious men in long black coats, round black hats, and white silk stockings also waited, hoping for an interview with the wise man holding court in a private room. More men milled about in front of the house where the sage met his faithful flock whenever he was in town.

A small boy with a pale, pointed face, dark hair, and sidecurls sat patiently next to his mother on a narrow bench. Today was a most special event, eight-year-old Eliezer Wiesel knew. Today was the day when the

Rabbi of Wishnitz visited his loyal followers in Elie's hometown as he did once a year, just before the High Holy Days. It seemed to the boy that this year's crowd of devout Hasidim who had come from near and far to be near their illustrious leader was the largest he had seen.

A feeling of joy and faith filled the streets, the neighborhood, the air. In these same Carpathian Mountains in whose foothills their town nestled the saintly Israel Baal Shem Tov, Master of the Good

View of Sighet's main square. (Reproduced with permission from the film Sighet, Sighet *by Harold Becker)*

Name, had once lived and taught. Here his words still had a home. From here his teachings had also spread to other Eastern European countries. A follower of the Baal Shem's beliefs was known as a Hasid, from the Hebrew word meaning "grace" or "piety." A Hasid believed that God was everywhere, that prayer and trust in God overcame the many problems of daily life. Hasidim celebrated their holidays with singing and dancing that left them feeling happy. They thought of their singing as a ladder that reached God.

Eliezer's mother brought him into town every year to receive the Rebbe's blessing. It was not usual for a woman to be a part of such an audience, certainly not in a community as strongly observant and religious as that of Sighet's Hasidim. But Eliezer knew even then that his mother was not an ordinary woman.

Sarah Wiesel was educated beyond the level of most of Sighet's Jewish women. Others could read and write, but she was one of the few Jewish girls who read several languages and was graduated from the local high school. The daughter of Dodye Feig, a highly regarded Hasid, and the wife of Shlomo Wiesel, well known as a businessman and community leader, Eliezer's mother was considered both bright and virtuous.

On this day Elie—or Leizer, as his family called him—watched in astonishment to see his mother approach the scribe who was writing *kvittlach* for visitors who wished to address the Rebbe but could not write them themselves.

Elie's large dark eyes grew even larger. Why did she need to pay a scribe? Especially since he knew she had already written out on a piece of paper the question she wished to ask the holy man. As if reading his thoughts, she smiled kindly. "The scribe needs the income, Elie. He depends on it."

"You may come in," said the caftaned old man who guarded the door. Grasping Elie's hand, Sarah led him into the room where the Wishnitzer Rebbe received his visitors. He was seated in a deep armchair. His wonderful white beard fanned out over his chest.

"Sarah, my dear child," he greeted Elie's mother with affection. He inquired about the family, especially about his old friend Dodye Feig, Elie's grandfather. The Rebbe had known Elie since the boy was very small, so it was natural for him to pick Elie up and hold him on his knee. Elie felt warm when the Rebbe smiled at him. The wise man reminded him of his beloved grandfather. That, too, was natural, for Dodye Feig was the Rebbe's favorite disciple.

After a while the Rebbe asked Sarah to leave the room so he might speak to Elie alone. He questioned Elie about his studies and about his interests. He nodded his head frequently over the enthusiastic, detailed answers. It seemed to Elie, however, that soon the wise man's smile faded, that his eyes turned cloudy with sadness.

When Sarah was requested to return to the room, it was Elie's turn to wait outside. He was there for only a little while. Soon his mother emerged from her audience with the Rebbe. She was crying softly, holding a handkerchief to her mouth. Without a word she took Elie by the hand and walked quickly through the crowded room and out the door. On the way home her tears increased. Soon she was sobbing so hard she couldn't speak. Elie was terribly upset.

"Did I do something bad, Mama?" he asked. He tried to remember whether he had given the Rebbe a wrong answer or had perhaps behaved improperly in some way.

Sarah shook her head and patted his shoulder to reassure him. "No, Leizer, you did well."

"But Mama, what is wrong?"

She walked faster and remained silent. After they crossed the threshold of their home on Serpent Street, Sarah disappeared into the bedroom and closed the door behind her. Elie stood outside the door, distressed and puzzled. What had his mother asked the Rebbe, he wondered. What had he, Elie, done to cause her tears?

After their last visit to the Rebbe of Wishnitz, Elie's mother cried frequently. Sometimes, when she felt herself unobserved, she looked at him with a strange expression on her face. It hurt him to think he had given her cause for worry.

To her son Sarah was the perfect mother: beautiful, warm, loving, and encouraging. He could bring her all his fears and she always knew how to turn them around in a hurry. Until now. Sarah never revealed to her son what the Rebbe had said when she questioned him about Elie's future. Not until many years later and far away from Sighet would Elie learn the exact words of the wise man's prophecy concerning him.

Sarah was a lively, dark-eyed, brown-haired woman who had been a beautiful and spirited young girl. Marriage, children, and her husband's business demanded much energy. Still, Sarah gave her only baby boy all the tender love he craved. Elie was born on September 30, 1928. That day happened to be Simhat Torah, the happy holiday meaning "Rejoicing of the Torah" which Jews celebrated with singing and dancing and wine, and she considered that a good omen. She had high hopes that she might transmit her deep religious faith to him and that Elie would grow up to be an observant Jew who believed in God. While he was still a baby she would sing him to sleep every night, and her sweet, melodious voice coaxed him into warm, restful slumber. When he grew too old for lullabies, she told him stories. A goat of gold, she said, will always be near your bed to watch over you. Even when you are grown and know all a grown man knows, he will still accompany you and guard you.

Elie thrived on her affection and her joyous manner. He was a melancholy, withdrawn boy, plagued by headaches, who was sometimes lonesome in the bustling household. He felt like an only child, except that he was not the only one. He had two sisters—Hilda and Bea—who were already old enough to join their mother in helping their father in his grocery store during the long hours he kept it open. But older sisters pay little attention to younger brothers, and

Elie as a young boy with his mother, Sarah, and his
two older sisters, Hilda and Bea.
(Reproduced with permission from the film
Sighet, Sighet *by Harold Becker)*

certainly they did not share the interests of the serious little boy who was so different from them.

It was fortunate that a close bond existed between mother and son, for Elie's father, Shlomo, was always busy, always running, but not often at home. A man who observed tradition but was not fanatic about religion, Shlomo was not involved in household affairs or in the raising of children. Nor in frequent visits to the synagogue. Highly educated and intelligent, he could often be found in government offices or in meeting halls where discussions affected the welfare of the community, both Jewish and Christian.

Shlomo Wiesel was a handsome, energetic man, clean-shaven except for a small, neatly trimmed mustache, with close-cropped dark hair receding from his high forehead. His eyes often had a serious, preoccupied look, but he was also able to enjoy life. Good food, good music, and intelligent conversation, these things made him happy and brought a smile to his full lips.

Elie did not see much of his father while he was a young child. He was proud that his father helped so many people in need. But he was always happy when Shlomo came home late at night, bringing small gifts of special fruits or sweets to his family.

A strong, practical person, Shlomo had an open mind. He lived for the present and tried to relieve the misfortunes he saw all around him. He was concerned about making a man of his son. He wanted the boy to grow up respecting and trusting his fellow man, in contrast to his wife and her family, more pious than he, who wanted to bring up Elie more deeply immersed in religion.

One day a week, on the Sabbath, Shlomo closed his store and walked with Elie to the little synagogue across the street from Sighet's market square. There he put on his prayer shawl and recited the prayers of the traditional Jew, his son by his side. Upon returning home, his Saturday afternoons were given over to his own personal studies. He read widely and kept himself informed on topics ranging from history to psychology. He insisted that his children, too, become interested in secular studies, especially modern languages, including the study of modern Hebrew, *Ivrit*.

Both parents were concerned over the frail health of their son. Pale and thin, Elie was taken to see various physicians in town and surrounding areas. No one diagnosed correctly the cause of his headaches or his weight loss. But then, no one knew Elie's secret. Twice a week, on Mondays and Thursdays, the boy fasted. On those days he refused to eat breakfast and the evening meal. And of course, only he knew why he fasted. He believed that by concentrating less on eating and more on his studies he was increasing his discipline and preparing for his future life. Elie was certain he would be either a rabbi or a teacher.

Sighet was actually only a small spot on the map of northern Transylvania, in the heart of the Balkans. But the tree-covered mountains that surrounded Sighet held treasures of ore and minerals, while in its fertile valleys grew large, life-sustaining food crops. Its natural wealth was constantly coveted by neighboring countries, and so Transylvania was alternately fought over and ruled by Hungary, Rumania, Austria, the Turkish Empire, Russia, and Germany. During Elie's childhood it belonged to Rumania.

Jews had lived in this region of long icy winters and short hot summers since the 1600s. Most of Sighet's Jewish citizens had always been very poor, yet all contributed in their way to the lifestyle of the town. During Elie's childhood a pulsing, thriving community of over ten thousand Jews called Sighet home, a generous one-third of the town's population. During the earliest years of his life Elie's every daily activity took place within a Jewish world. All the people he knew: his family, his teachers, the doctors, the people who offered their wares at the weekly market, everyone was Jewish. His knowledge of the outside world was limited.

Already early in life he noticed that the windows and doors of Jewish homes were shuttered tight at the times Christians celebrated their holidays of Christmas and Easter. His parents made every effort to shield him from stories of vandalism and bodily attacks on Jews by drunk peasants roaming the area. Shlomo was a realistic, practical man who worked hard to establish respect between the Christians and Jews of his town. He did not dwell on such incidents and did not like to hear of them in his home. Yet the tales filtered down to Elie and frightened him. As he grew older he accepted such persecution almost as a law of nature, knowing that it was safer for a Jew not to be in the street while his neighbors observed Christmas or Easter.

Elie was only three years old when his mother enrolled him in *cheder*, the traditional Jewish primary school where little boys learned the Hebrew alphabet which would become the key to later studies of the Holy Books. Elie was very unhappy. He thought only about being separated from his mother and worried about being pushed out of the house. Almost every morning he invented a new ailment, hoping that by being ill he might be allowed to stay home from school one more day.

His teachers were old men from neighboring villages, beginning with the first one who taught him the Hebrew *aleph, bet, gimel* in the darkness of some dusty nook which served as the classroom for the local Jewish children. As Elie was to write many years later in his memoir, *Legends of Our Time*, it was "the teacher from Betize" who "was the first to speak to me lovingly about language. He put his heart and soul into each syllable, each punctuation mark."

At age six, long after Elie and his classmates had mastered the letters, another teacher, "Zeide, the Melamed," introduced them to the writings of the Bible. The following year, when Elie was seven, the same teacher taught them Rashi's commentaries. At eight, Elie and his classmates entered the world of the oral tradition, which meant that their teacher, Itzhak—the Melamed's assistant—read them a passage from the Talmud, which the boys repeated, chanting in unison until they had it memorized. Elie was extremely proud when at the end of that semester he could absorb and retain a whole page of text a week. He stayed with Itzhak for two years until he was ten years old, and then became the student of the "Selishter Rebbe," a man so unhappy and brutal that his pupils felt terrorized by him.

Every one of his teachers opened doors of knowledge and enrichment to him, yet Elie found their personalities and teaching methods strange, often frightening. These troubled, moody men were not joyful and the long daytime hours spent in dark uncomfortable school rooms were hard. Not until he was twelve years old did Elie find several enlightened and tolerant teachers in neighboring villages who treated him and his fellow students as intelligent, somewhat grown-up boys who enjoyed the new knowledge opening up to them.

2

Dodye Feig

The person to whom little Elie felt the closest was Dodye Feig, his maternal grandfather. Dodye's real name was David, or Dovid in Hebrew, but because many people felt affectionate toward him it became "little David."

Elie thought of his grandfather as the "true Hasid." Dodye became the symbol of everything the boy admired about Hasidism. Small in stature, but wiry, ruddy-cheeked, with a long white beard, Dodye was the Wishnitzer Rebbe's favorite disciple.

Unfortunately Elie saw his grandfather all too seldom. Dodye lived in a tiny village seven kilometers outside Sighet where he owned a small farm and operated his grocery store. It was not nearly often enough for Elie that he came to Sighet to share a Shabbat or holiday dinner with his daughter and her family. But when he heard Dodye's joyful voice chant the blessings and pray with fervor and conviction, Elie believed that their white-clad holiday table had become an altar where angels hid in the shadows. According to Dodye, angels were present wherever faithful Jews observed the Sabbath. Elie's grandfather sang beautifully, and his voice expressed all the feeling that a good Jew has for his God. A special brand of holiness surrounded the whole family when Dodye sang. It was a celebration when he led them through the Sabbath at the Wiesel home.

The old man had had a hard life. Even now he worked harder than most younger men. He was known by all his fellow villagers. Jew and Gentile alike admired and respected him for his humanity toward everyone. In his grocery store he extended credit when money was tight. He gave food to those he knew to be hungry. He scolded the peasants when they drank too much or when they beat their wives.

Elie appreciated him most because Dodye listened. He did not treat his grandson's problems as childish, but put them on an equal level with those of adults. Dodye neither chided nor corrected. He *knew* when something troubled Elie. He truly understood. Best of all, a little talk with Dodye relieved it all.

Dodye's visits to Sighet and to the little hasidic synagogue across the street from their house were a delight to Elie. He was so proud of the way Dodye sang. All the praying men in black stopped their chanting long enough to listen and smile happily.

Dodye wore his special silk holiday caftan and the fur-bordered hat reserved for important occasions. Elie felt the warmth and kinship during the services. He felt the joy and gratitude of the worshippers offering their prayers to God. He felt that he was one of them, even though he was only a little boy who with his *payes* and skullcap was but a miniature of the others. For Elie, this joy was the essence of Judaism. This feeling of belonging was what it meant to be a Jew. He felt at home.

Dodye was the source of many legends, primarily about the Baal Shem and other hasidic masters. Elie retained many of them. Later in his life he retold them in his writings. As a child he especially liked one saying attributed to the Baal Shem: "God sees, God watches. He is in every life, in every thing. The world hinges on His will." It made Elie feel good to hear such stories. It was wonderful to think that God controlled every action and every deed in a person's life. All one had to do was to believe in Him—firmly and devotedly—and things would go right in the whole world.

There were times when a startling feeling overcame Elie. They occurred most frequently while he was praying with Dodye in Sighet's hasidic synagogue, his grandfather at his side, surrounded by the pious, chanting men, so fervent and devoted. It was then that Elie felt God was speaking directly to him. He believed that his prayers established a personal link with God. So strong was this feeling that he believed God might even grant all the wishes Elie had for himself and for others.

"I believed profoundly," he would later say of those days in which he felt that nothing was impossible and that his own intense prayers might even bring the Messiah.

Elie was seven years old when his little sister Tsiporah was born. Despite his delight in this sweet, dainty baby, he felt even more lonely than before. Working parents, older sisters, and a new baby—there was less time than before devoted to him.

One day when he felt especially low Elie started out to visit the one person who loved him best and understood him fully. His mother had taken him to see Dodye on previous occasions, so Elie knew in what general direction his grandfather's village lay. It was a distance of seven kilometers. The small boy walked for many hours until he reached the countryside. Reb Dodye's eyebrows rose sharply at the sight of Elie as he entered the farm house and fell exhaustedly into a chair. He did not reprimand the boy. Instead, he sent word to his daughter by the next coachman traveling to Sighet that the boy was safe.

Not until after the evening prayers and the meal were finished did his grandfather ask why Elie had come.

"I missed you very much, grandfather."

"That's all? No trouble at school? At home?"

"No, grandfather."

Sensing the boy's loneliness, Dodye spoke of other things. He confessed that in his childhood days he, too, had run away from home when he needed advice and reassurance. Only he had run to his rebbe, who had helped him to see things right.

Elie did not need the rebbe. When he felt sad or misunderstood he sought shelter with Dodye. Being with his grandfather was all the tonic he needed. He knew he was loved and Dodye's vigor and joy made him happy.

It was always difficult to say goodbye to Dodye. Whenever his mother took him to visit his grandfather,

Elie and his younger sister, Tsiporah, with their mother. (Reproduced with permission from the film Sighet, Sighet *by Harold Becker)*

the farewell was a painful moment underlined by Elie's tears. Usually it was the moment when Dodye bent down to him and smilingly reminded him, "Look at me and you won't cry." On only one occasion was the goodbye different.

It was early in the spring of 1944. Dodye had spent the Sabbath with the family in Sighet. As he was leaving on Sunday morning, ready to climb into his horse-drawn wagon for the return trip, he bent over Elie for a final word. "You are Jewish, your task is to remain Jewish. The rest is up to God." It was the last time Elie saw his grandfather.

3

Moshe's Story

Twelve-year-old Elie was troubled by the talk he heard around him. In the 1940s rumors of the possibility of war and the threat of an invasion by Germany into Hungary swirled everywhere. Among friends of the family, at the synagogue when he went with Shlomo, people asked, "What will happen to us if … ?" It was a question never finished, for there was no answer, or at least none that anyone wished to give.

Elie was most disturbed by the demeanor of his mother. Sarah had never quite recovered her own optimism and vitality after their visit to the Rebbe of Wishnitz. She was serious most of the time now and her eyes looked clouded, almost turned inward as if she, too, were searching for an answer. One Shabbat

Elie heard her say at table, "Why couldn't we leave and go to Palestine?" The question was directed at Shlomo, but was said almost as if she were asking herself, almost as if she knew that bringing up the subject was a hopeless, useless proposition.

"Why should we leave?" His father's voice was harsh. "We have nothing to fear here. Jews have lived in Sighet since the seventeenth century. Everyone knows us here, knows our family. Nothing will happen to us." After that, Sarah never brought up the topic again. Perhaps she felt it was useless to discuss it.

Though he heard and felt threatening vibrations around him, Elie did not realize they would affect him and forgot them when studying. Even though Elie was a full-time religious school student, Shlomo felt his son should have a good general education and had registered him in the state high school system as soon as he reached the age of twelve. To advance from one grade to the next, a student in the Hungarian school system had to take a yearly examination to prove he was qualified. Elie concentrated on his religious studies for ten months during the year, then "crammed" his secular studies of Latin, mathematics, and physics into one month. Every December Elie and Shlomo traveled about eighty miles by train westward to the Rumanian regional capital of Debrecen, where Elie was tested.

Latin was one of the requirements for which Elie was responsible. Fortunately, a good Latin teacher lived in Sighet who tutored Elie and some of his friends. The lady owned a phonograph—one of the very few in town—and as a reward for their diligence in learning Latin she allowed her better students to use it. Elie always arrived at his lessons heavily laden. Not only did he bring his exercise books, but he carried the phonograph records he had bought with his small allowance and longed to hear. Sitting in his teacher's living room listening to recordings by the famous cantors of his day brought him moments of supreme pleasure and confirmed him as an ardent music lover for life. The pleasure even spurred him on during the three violin lessons per week given to Elie by a friendly policeman at the station across the street from his home.

It was a very full program for a young schoolboy. Yet Elie's thirst for learning was not satisfied. The little boy who read constantly had turned into a young boy deeply immersed in the legends and mysteries of Jewish learning. Books were food for his soul: he devoured them. Even his Talmudic studies were not enough. He studied from early morning to late at night, far more than his schoolmates.

Elie longed to find answers to questions that no scholar had yet found. When will the persecution of the Jewish people stop? Why is there no peace in the world? When will the Messiah come? Just as at times he felt that his prayers were heard by God, and that he might be the person to bring the Messiah, so Elie felt that somewhere there were answers to the questions that obsessed him. If only he could delve into the unknown writings of Judaism. There was one book, he knew, that contained the lore and teachings of Jewish mysticism. These were the keys which opened the secret meaning behind every letter and word in the Bible.

"Please find me a master who can teach me to understand Kabbalah," he begged his father.

The request did not surprise Shlomo. He knew of Elie's melancholy moods, his obsession with prayers, and his questions about the existence of God. He felt that Elie's approaching adolescence might be to blame for such thoughts. But studying the Kabbalah—that was going too far. Suddenly Shlomo felt very nervous about young Elie wanting to explore the secrets contained in that ancient book.

"You are much too young," he said. "Grown men study the Kabbalah, not young boys not yet Bar Mitzvah. Besides, there is no one here in Sighet qualified to teach you." With that Shlomo thought he had dismissed the subject.

Near the end of 1940, when Elie was twelve years old, he found his own teacher. His name was Moshe. Moshe was the caretaker at the synagogue to which Elie frequently went after school hours. Moshe was middle-aged and poor, dressed in ragged clothes; he often walked barefoot. He was an extremely shy man with awkward, clumsy movements. No one actually knew his last name, where he had come from, or whether he had a family. It was obvious to everyone in the community that Moshe did not quite fit into anyone's social life. Some said he was mentally defective. Others, more kindly, pitied him and merely thought him odd. Yet his large eyes, his timid smile, and his gift for singing endeared him to many of Sighet's Jews.

Moshe became Elie's second adult friend. Just like Dodye Feig, Moshe treated him like an equal and considered his thoughts with respect. Perhaps it flattered him to have the full attention of a young person; perhaps he enjoyed being needed by Elie as a guide during their many hours of discussion about God, which often lasted until late at night. Elie could speak freely to him on topics he found troubling and know that he was taken seriously by an adult.

Elie spoke with Moshe about many things: God, humankind, and the relationship between them. One evening he spoke of his desire to study the Kabbalah and the difficulties of finding a teacher. Moshe offered to be his guide and began reading the Book of Splendor—the Zohar—with him. From then on they sat together almost every evening and read by candlelight in the caretaker's little room at the back of the synagogue.

Shlomo had feared that Elie's search into the Jewish past, conducted in the ghostly darkness of deserted buildings, was unhealthy for a young boy. Instead, Elie found that it led him into a newly discovered world of brightness and knowledge. Night after night they read out loud together. They went over each passage slowly until the meaning of every word became clear. Elie found answers to many of the questions he had been asking. The Book of Splendor revealed to him the presence of God in everything, both good and evil. Everything had its order in the universe. Every human being carried inside him or her a touch of the divine, a spark that yearned to be united with God, who was the source of life and light. All that was required of humans to achieve this unity was intense prayer, the practice of God's commandments, and love and kindness for all living beings.

Elie was happier than he had ever been. He was doing what his inner self told him he must do: find answers to his questions about God and the universe. At the same time in the world beyond the Carpathian Mountains plans were being made to destroy those answers forever.

In the fall of 1941, when he reached the age of thirteen, Elie became a Bar Mitzvah. During a weekday service at the small hasidic synagogue in Sighet where he worshipped with Dodye Feig whenever his grandfather came into town, the rabbi honored him by helping Elie put on his first set of tefillin, the two small leather cases a devout Jew binds to his forehead and his left arm during morning prayers. Now he was considered an adult and responsible for his own actions. To mark the special occasion, his parents presented Elie with a golden pocket watch.

During the following months, while Elie and Moshe continued to spend their evenings studying by the light of one candle, major political changes occurred in Europe which would soon affect them. Since September 1, 1939, when Germany invaded Poland and World War II began, rumors and fears had circulated among the Jewish citizens of Sighet. In

1940 Germany had taken half of Transylvania from Rumania and given it to Hungary. Sighet now belonged to Hungary, which was a partner in the Germany-Italy-Japan "Axis." Soon afterward the local Fascist party took over the government of Hungary. In 1941 Hungary began passing race laws depriving Jews of their citizenship rights.

Germany began to carry out the first phase of its program of Jewish extermination by rounding up twenty thousand "alien" Jews in Hungary and sending them to Poland, where they were executed. Most of the Jews still living in Hungary were unaware of this action, believing that the exiled "aliens" had been resettled in labor camps. When news of the killings slowly trickled back to them, their fears intensified. They knew their own bad times were coming closer.

In Sighet anti-Jewish feelings by neighbors were displayed more openly than before. Food shortages that were actually due to the war were blamed on the Jews. On the radio and in newspapers anti-Semitic articles became daily features. Jews were beaten up in the streets by Hungarian rowdies.

Elie knew his world was changing on the day Hungarian gendarmes came to arrest Shlomo Wiesel at his grocery store. Shlomo was charged with helping Polish Jews escape over the border into Hungary. His sentence was two months in jail. Elie saw his mother and older sisters run the family store in the father's absence, their eyes full of fear, their lips tight with worry. Would his father return? What would happen next?

Shlomo returned haggard, thin, and tired. He never spoke of his ordeal to his family, but soon resumed his frequent short absences. The whispers Elie often heard coming from his parents' room late at night convinced him that his father was once more engaged in helping Polish Jews escape over the border.

Early one gray dawn, Elie experienced for himself what it all meant—the fear, the whispers, the rumors. A sudden new law had come down from the Hungarian government that all foreign Jews had to leave Sighet. At once. Without needing to be told, he knew that meant Moshe, who was not from Sighet and had no papers that proved where he came from. He was considered an "alien," a foreigner.

Elie rose early the next day and walked to the train station, hoping to say a silent goodbye to Moshe. His friend stood amid other alien Jews already lined up under the watchful eyes of the armed Hungarian police who supervised the deportation. Pale with shock and emotion, the young boy tried to wave to him, but Moshe's arms were filled with parcels and he could not wave back. Many Jewish townspeople had come to bring food packages to those who were forced to leave. All were weeping, those forced to leave and those who stayed behind. Elie trembled and tears blurred his vision as he stood on the station platform and saw pistol- and club-bearing troops push his friend and teacher into a boxcar that would take him out of his life.

By 1943 life was even harder for Elie and the Jews in Sighet. Many months had passed and he still missed

Moshe, especially during evening hours. Now he hurried home quickly after the brief daily *maariv* service, before the synagogue was totally empty and its dark shadows reminded him of his missing master.

But he never stopped studying after Moshe left. He did not read the Kabbalah, because, as his father had predicted, there were no qualified teachers in Sighet. He had already discovered how true was the advice in *Pirke avot* (The Sayings of the Fathers): The best way to study is to find a teacher and learn together with a friend.

Instead of learning Kabbalah, he now studied Talmud with the father of a friend and prayed before and after the early morning class. Studying comforted him and lulled him into an illusion of safety. After all, didn't the Talmud say, "Whoever occupies himself with Torah, keeps suffering at a distance"?

One evening during the fall months of 1943 Elie walked into a *maariv* service when in the dark shadows at the rear of the synagogue he saw a familiar figure. He could not believe it. Moshe! His dear friend and teacher had returned! With the greatest joy he ran to the back and embraced the former caretaker, longing to know what had happened to him and how he had managed to come back. But to his dismay he discovered that this unkempt, disheveled person was not the Moshe he had known. Gentle, dreamy-eyed Moshe had become a tormented creature, restless and bizarre, who talked endlessly. He stopped everyone, frantic to tell his story.

The boxcar in which Moshe and his fellow deportees were taken out of Sighet traveled for many hours until it reached a forest in Galicia, near Kolomaye, where German soldiers took over from the Hungarian police guards. The train was emptied. Everyone was marched to a big ditch and ordered to line up single file. Suddenly soldiers on the other side of the ditch raised their guns and fired. Moshe saw one after another of the deportees fall into the ditch, dead. He, too, fell, wounded in the leg. He felt a heavy weight and knew that one of the bodies had fallen on him, covering him. He lay there pretending to be dead until the soldiers finally withdrew. When darkness came, Moshe managed to climb out of the ditch and fled into the countryside.

For many days people listened to Moshe sympathetically. During this time Elie did not leave Moshe's side. Moshe tried frantically to reach every Jewish person, pulling people by their sleeve to make them hear his story. But as the days passed interest in his stories faded.

Moshe was heartbroken. "I came back to warn them," he said. His tears ran over his unshaven cheeks. "My only purpose in escaping death was to let people here know what lies ahead so they can save themselves. And now they don't even believe me."

Elie was saddened and shocked when he saw how little effect Moshe's terrible story had on the Jews of Sighet. People still listened and shook their heads and clucked their tongues, but then they went on with their daily business and it was as if nothing had ever happened.

4

The Face in the Window

Moshe's story had a terrifying effect on Elie. He had many sleepless nights during which he wondered why the Germans had killed the foreign Jews from Sighet. As he tossed in his bed, he worried what lay ahead for those still in the town, but he was especially perturbed at the indifference of the local Jews about their future. He could not understand it.

One fall night in 1943 he waited for his father to come home, determined to speak with him. He sat quietly while Shlomo, gray and weary, ate a late supper. Everything about him seemed downcast. His father had looked noticeably older in recent months. It was not easy for Elie to talk about such a difficult topic, especially to his father, but now he felt it was his duty. He took a deep breath to gather sufficient courage and said, "Father, why can't we leave Sighet and go to Palestine while there is still time?"

Shlomo raised his head. "Why?"

Elie faltered, just a little. "I think every Jew's dream is someday to live in Palestine."

Shlomo thought for a moment. "For me it is too late to move to another country and start life over," he said. "If you want to go to Palestine, go."

"Alone?"

His father nodded his head.

Both Elie and his mother had tried unsuccessfully to persuade him. It was the last time anyone spoke of moving the family out of Sighet.

In the spring of 1944 Elie enjoyed the good smells of simmering chicken soup, potato and onion kugels, and knaidels made of matzoh meal, and watched his mother and sisters prepare for Passover, which occurred early that year, in March. It had always been a time of much work and great anticipation in the family. The girls usually chattered about new clothes, hoped for good spring weather, and gossiped happily about boyfriends, while Sarah Wiesel worked with Maria, their Christian maid, cleaning out cupboards, switching their daily dishes for special holiday ones, and removing all traces of *chometz*—leavened baked goods—from the kitchen.

Despite the activities of their household getting ready for an important holiday, nothing was the same as in other years. Elie sensed it, everyone sensed it. Radio Budapest had announced that on March 19,

1944 Germany had occupied all of Hungary. A strong sense of foreboding hung over the entire Jewish community. The first blow came with the dreaded knock on house doors at dawn of the last day of Passover. Leaders of the Sighet Jewish community were dragged out of their houses and brought to the town square. There the German commandant barked at them and told them that all future orders would come from him and had better be obeyed. A few of the coatless men shivering with fear in the early April mountain air noticed the special insignia—a death's head—on his black uniform. They realized that the commandant and his men were not regular German soldiers but members of a unit called the Waffen SS, about whom dreadful rumors had already reached Sighet.

Three days later a house search followed. Hungarian policemen working with the Germans went from door to door, searching for gold, silver, jewelry, and money—whatever valuables they found in Jewish homes—and taking it all away. Anyone not turning over these items was subject to the death penalty.

Elie saw his father handing over all their precious belongings and felt sick. He thought of his golden Bar Mitzvah watch, hidden among his school books. What if it was discovered?

After three days of house arrest Sighet's Jews were allowed to come out again, after each person had sewn on his or her clothing a large yellow star about the size of the palm of one's hand that identified that person as a Jew.

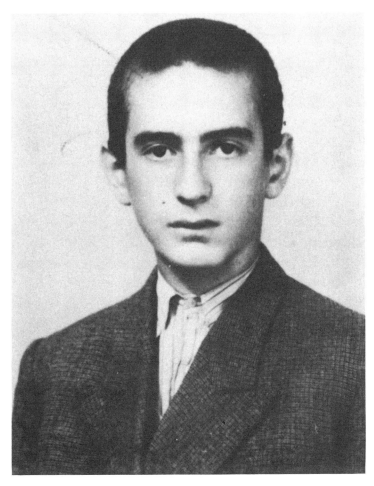

*Elie as a schoolboy of fifteen in Sighet prior to
deportation.
(Courtesy of Elie Wiesel and Elirion, Inc.)*

Now almost every day brought a new edict and
more restrictions from the Germans. Each one was
designed to tighten the noose around the town's Jews
a little closer. Every Jewish family could only live in
one of two areas designated especially as ghettos and

sealed by barbed wire every night so that no one could escape. The Wiesels were lucky. They lived in a large corner home in the center of town within one of the designated ghetto areas and they did not have to move.

On a warm Saturday night in June 1944, shortly before the holiday of Shavuot, Sighet's Jews received word that they would be moving out of town the following morning. The dreaded pronouncement—DEPORTATION—came two and a half months after the German arrival, just as everyone had been lulled into believing that things could not get worse, that this was as far as the Germans would go.

Elie was one of the young boys acting as "runners" who moved from house to house that sleepless night, to make sure everyone in the community knew of the forthcoming event and would be ready to go. Baggage was restricted to what everyone could carry. The destination was unknown.

The night hours were filled with indescribable panic. The ghetto streets were quickly littered with discarded belongings as people frantically selected what to take and what to leave behind. Mothers packed food for their families to take on a journey of uncertain length. In the darkness people buried jewelry and silver in the soil of their gardens. Elie saw his father dig a hole in their backyard to hide the jewelry he had kept from the German house search. He watched in silence as his mother interred her silver Sabbath candlesticks. That is when he decided that he, too, would bury the treasure he valued most: his

Bar Mitzvah watch. Near a tree in the rear of the garden he placed the box that contained the beloved pocket watch in a small hole which he covered carefully. Someday, he was certain, he would return, locate the spot, and be reunited with his most prized possession.

What struck Elie most about the next day, a late April Sunday in 1944, was its silence. It was a church day in Sighet and normally quiet, but the scene before him made it seem all the more incredible that there was so little noise. The Jews of Sighet stood lined up in front of their houses, their few belongings piled up near them or in their hands, ready to leave. They had been standing like that since dawn when the Hungarian police, lists in hand, had knocked on every door and yelled for the occupants to come out. Many hours had passed while the policemen checked and re-checked their lists. The sun was hot and bright over them, and still they stood, young and old, parents and children. And all were silent.

Heat and exhaustion overcame the very old and the very young, and they sank down on their baggage without a sound.

When after the endless list-checking the line of people finally began to move, most of the day had gone by. Through his connections as an official of the Jewish community, Shlomo learned that, since their name was near the end of the alphabet, the Wiesels would not move out that day, but could stay in their house for at least another day, perhaps two. So the family stood, all of them, behind their garden fence, and watched as the silent line filed by. In that line were all the faces familiar to them. Elie felt his whole childhood move past him as one by one he recognized his old teachers, rabbis, and family friends.

Those in-between days until the final departure from the town felt dreamlike to Elie, for nothing that occurred made any sense. Not why they were being sent away, nor the manner in which it was being done. On the final night in his own bed he tried to think of all the things he wanted to remember about his home. He feared that once he was homeless he would no longer matter as a person.

He rose earlier than usual the next day and prayed even before sunrise. It was important to him to put on his phylacteries and go through the whole ritual, especially on this day. It gave him peace. By the time he heard the police outside yelling, "All Jews out," he was ready and was the first of his family to step over the threshold into the street. He did not turn around to look at his family, afraid he would cry if he saw their tears. And he did not want to cry. But once he was outside and had to bend down to pick up his bag, he glanced at his father and saw that he was crying. It was the first time he had seen Shlomo, the strict father, the strong, firm advisor, the respected community leader, cry. It shocked Elie more than the whole idea of leaving Sighet did. His father's tears hurt him deeply.

What hurt the most however, was the loud silence that hung over the town. Those who were leaving filed around the market square and passed the houses of their Christian neighbors with whom they had shared a lifetime in Sighet. Now no one was to be seen. Not one hand lifted to wave goodbye. Elie was greatly troubled. He knew that behind their windows the townspeople were watching the exodus of one-fourth of Sighet's population. In silence.

The idea that people could witness such an injustice in total apathy distressed Elie deeply that day. That distress always remained with him. How could anyone just *watch*? A person who just watches silently without a whisper of protest while other living beings suffer is guilty of indifference. Indifference is a sin. A sin as great, he felt, as actively engaging in an evil deed.

Much later in his life Elie wrote a story he called "The Face in the Window." He included the story in one of his novels, *The Town Beyond the Wall*. In the story he describes a person who just watches, a silent witness. Almost as if recalling a memory of that leave-taking day in Sighet, Elie pictures a man hiding behind the curtains of his window. A man who observes without comment, expression, or feeling the events taking place in the street. It might have been an imaginary figure he was describing, but that face in the window was to become Elie's symbol of a person, a nation, a world's inertia in the face of evil. Though he did not know it when he left Sighet as a youngster, for Elie overcoming the "I-don't-want-to-get-involved" feeling of the silent watchers began on the day he and all the Jews of his hometown were deported.

5

Entering the Kingdom of Night

It took a full week—from Sunday to Saturday—to move the thousands of people from their homes to the train station. The Jews of Sighet spent their last twenty-four hours in town in the main synagogue. They consoled themselves with rumors that their next destination would be a work camp in the center of Hungary where they would stay until the war was over.

The Wiesel family was in the last group which stood on the station platform and faced the long row of freight cars waiting to be loaded. Black-clad SS men again read off lists, counting off eighty persons per car. Elie huddled close to his father. His greatest fear was being separated from his family.

Elie had never traveled out of town before, except

Sighet's main synagogue.
(Reproduced with permission from the film
Sighet, Sighet *by Harold Becker)*

for short vacation trips by train with his family to nearby mountain resorts or the longer yearly train ride to Debrecen for his school examinations. Whatever his expectations may have been, this train ride was different. The eighty people who shared the tight space huddled on the floor of the freight car, trying to stay within family groups for safety and reassurance. The food they had brought along was soon eaten. The extreme summer heat made them thirsty. Two water buckets—one on each side of the car— were quickly used up. Without sanitary facilities people had to relieve themselves in the corners of the car

*Jews' Street in Sighet after its occupants were deported.
(Reproduced with permission from the film*
Sighet, Sighet *by Harold Becker)*

while their fellow travelers tried to look away.

Elie thought of Maria, their maid of many years, who had to leave them when the Jews were forced to live in ghettos and were no longer allowed to have Christians work for them. Just a few days previously the faithful old woman had knocked on their door and offered the family a refuge in her mountain hut outside town. Perhaps she had heard rumors of what lay ahead. Shlomo had thanked her but refused her offer. As an official of the Jewish community he felt he was needed in town and should remain there with his wife and little Tsiporah. Did Elie and the older girls wish to go with Maria? the father asked. No one wished to respond with a "yes" if it meant leaving the family.

Elie also thought of Moshe, his master and friend. He recalled hearing that someone had seen Moshe running down the street on that terrible night when the deportation was first announced. According to the witness, the caretaker had been wild-eyed, crying, "I told you, I told you," before disappearing into the shadows of the night. No one had seen him since. Elie hoped with all his heart that Moshe had gotten away.

After a few hours of travel the train stopped at a small station someone recognized as near the Czechoslovakian border. A terrible hush fell on all inside the car. They were not traveling in the expected direction—toward the interior of Hungary and the work camp where they would spend time until the war's end. Instead they were leaving Hungary behind! Suddenly their train door opened. A German army officer strode in and barked that from now on they were under the jurisdiction of the German army. The last illusion evaporated at that moment. Now they had to face their worst fears.

After four days and nights of travel the train halted. Someone near a crack in the side of the freight car read a sign. It was in German and said "Auschwitz." No one had ever heard that name before.

The train stood still that whole day. When night

came, it moved forward again, but only for a little while. Then it stopped. They had arrived at Birkenau, reception center for the larger camp of Auschwitz.

It was midnight. From inside the freight car Elie could see bright flames, flames that seemed to come from a nearby high chimney stack. Almost immediately he smelled a sickening odor. He didn't know what it was. Then he heard someone in the car whisper in a voice of disbelief, "It's flesh, it's the smell of burning human flesh."

Before that thought had registered, the doors slid open. Gangs of men in striped tunics and dark trousers shone big flashlights on the car's dazed occupants, and yelled, "Schnell, schnell" ("fast, fast") to hurry them out. They pulled out those who did not move fast enough and swung their clubs, hitting everyone within reach.

Within minutes everyone in Elie's car stood on the large platform, blinking and confused. All around them were black-clad SS men with guns drawn, holding growling dogs. A loud voice ordered them to form two lines, men to the left, women to the right. Again voices shouted "Schnell, schnell," commanding them to hurry. It seemed nothing ever moved at a regular pace.

Elie saw his mother and his sisters move away from him. His mother was holding eight-year-old Tsiporah by the hand and stroking the child's hair with her free hand to calm her. He saw her walking in the long line of women and girls to his right. As in a dream, she soon disappeared from his sight. He did not know then that the right line led directly to the gas chambers and that he would never see his mother or Tsiporah again. Elie clung tightly to Shlomo's arm, determined not to become separated from him, too. In that second he knew instinctively that they would have to stay together to survive.

It was long past midnight at Birkenau. Walking in a row of five abreast with his father next to him, Elie became part of a huge crowd of men heading down a long road. On the right stood the empty freight trains that had brought the prisoners here. On their left a high electrified barbed-wire fence ran behind a deep ditch as far as the eye could see. Ahead of them several tall smokestacks spewed bright-burning flames into the night.

On either side of the moving row, veteran prisoners in striped black and white garb stirred in the shadows and yelled at the newcomers, warning them they would be burned in the furnaces looming in front of them. One man even jumped in front of Elie and asked his age.

"Fifteen," he said.

"No, no, eighteen, you fool," the hoarse voice shouted before the man disappeared again in darkness. Another man warned Shlomo to lower his age from fifty to forty before he, too, was swallowed in the shadows.

Later Elie was to discover that these warnings, brutal as they were, had been well meant in an effort to save their lives. Now, however, everything that was happening was nightmarish and unreal. Behind him

Elie heard whispered voices of protest from the younger men in line, some of whom carried knives. "Let us try to fight," these voices said angrily. "We won't allow them to kill us without a fight." But he also heard other, older voices pleading for reason. "Do not lose faith, even with the sword over our heads." Most of all, however, he heard the sentiment: "Wait until the world hears what is really happening at Auschwitz."

They finally reached a center square. In the middle of it stood yet another black-clad SS officer. In one eye he wore a monocle. His hand held a baton with which he determined the fate of each new arrival. This was the infamous Dr. Josef Mengele. As each prisoner reached him, the SS man asked a few curt questions. He pointed the baton to the right or the left and the prisoner had to move into the corresponding line.

When Elie stepped up to Dr. Mengele, he was asked: "Age?" and answered "Eighteen." To the question "Occupation?" he answered "Farmer." The baton pointed to the left. Anxiously Elie checked to see whether his father was in that same line, and was relieved that he was. He did not know whether left or right meant life or death. The important thing was to be with his father, no matter what happened.

He soon learned that left meant life, and that those designated to the right were judged unfit for labor and were to be killed almost immediately on arrival.

Elie and his father moved on. They reached a blazing pit ahead of them and Elie remembered the words of the men who had yelled at them a short while before. He thought that the time had come when he and his father would die. Instead they saw a large truck pull up and empty its cargo into the burning pit. To his utter horror he saw that the cargo consisted of babies and little children!

As a devout Jewish boy who had spent most of his life in study and prayer, Elie presumed that a special relationship existed between God and those who believed in Him. And yet here in front of him was a situation that canceled out everything he had been taught. How could human beings burn alive little children? *How could his god allow such a deed to occur?*

He looked at Shlomo, hoping that his father, who had always been able to make things right for others, would speak to him and assure him that what he was seeing was not true. He wanted to hear his father say that Elie was having nightmares and should wake up. But Shlomo himself appeared dazed. His lips were moving, his shoulders shaking with sobs. He mumbled that apparently the world did not care what was happening to them, that it had forsaken them.

Elie heard voices uttering words all around him. He saw lips move and recognized the words. Every man in the group, including Shlomo, was reciting Kaddish, the Hebrew prayer for the dead. But instead of saying it for someone who had died previously, they were saying it for themselves, knowing there would be no one left to follow them who would perform this mitzvah for them.

In that instant Elie knew that their roles had

reversed. Shlomo's trust in the goodness of human beings had collapsed. From now on Elie would have to be the one to support and reassure his father.

Just as the new arrivals reached the burning pit, more SS men appeared and directed them toward the barracks ahead of them. Instinctively Elie knew that for now they were spared a fiery death. The group trudged on in silence.

That first night was the hardest. It seemed endless. The men were admitted in groups of five hundred into wooden barracks that resembled horse stalls. The layers of wood slats ringed both sides of the building. These were the intended sleeping quarters for one thousand people. But on this night no one was allowed to sleep.

First, the prisoners were ordered to strip naked. Again, truncheon blows hit those who did not obey fast enough. Then, leaving their clothing behind, the men had to run to another part of the barracks where they were driven through hot showers, followed by applications of strong disinfectants. Shivering in the night air, they stood outside in rows while SS officers circulated among them, studying the nude prisoners. This was the second Selection they underwent that night. Dr. Mengele and his life-or-death decision had been the first. Now the SS were choosing the strongest looking men for special duties. Later on Elie found out that these men, handpicked by the SS, were going to work in the crematoria, a job they would not do for long before they themselves were killed.

From the many hours of standing in the cold without any food or cover, Elie's father developed severe stomach cramps. Finally in desperation he walked out of his row and up to their guard, a mean-tempered gypsy. Politely Shlomo asked him in German where the toilets were. Without a word the guard looked him up and down several times, raised his fist, and knocked Shlomo to the ground. Horrified, Elie stood in his place and witnessed his father lying motionless on the ground. Elie's face flooded with shame. He had watched his father being degraded and not done anything about it! Was it not his duty to defend his father by knocking down the guard? But he had done nothing and now he was overcome by guilt. Only a few hours in this camp and already he had changed. It helped little to have Shlomo get up, rub his face, and tell Elie that it really hadn't hurt too much.

Finally, the new men were marched to yet another barracks in the compound, where they were issued prison clothing. Dawn came, and still no one had been allowed to sleep or even sit on the ground to rest. Elie did not know it then, but he had already learned a vital lesson of camp life from Shlomo. Be inconspicuous, draw no attention to yourself. It may save your life!

On that first dreary morning in Auschwitz, as Elie was marched toward Building #17—his new home—he felt a heavy, greasy rain falling on him. The slow, thick rain smelled and tasted of bitter almonds. He looked up and saw the smokestacks in the near distance belching brownish-black clouds that hovered over the whole camp. With a heavy heart he wished he didn't know what the chimneys were burning.

At Auschwitz prisoners were housed in two-story concrete buildings instead of the wooden barracks at Birkenau. The compound consisted of acres and acres of such constructions, separated from one another by more electrified barbed wire.

Once again the prisoners underwent the showers and the disinfecting procedure. Elie learned this was a routine that would be followed every time inmates were moved from one location to another.

The next morning, when everyone assembled for outside roll call, the men were told to roll up their sleeves. Afterward one row after another walked past a small table were three veteran prisoners manned tattoo needles. When his turn came, a man engraved a number inside Elie's left forearm. Elie Wiesel lost his name and became prisoner #A-7713. From then on that number was his only identification. Whether it was to answer the daily roll call or to report to a camp authority, it would be only by number.

Shlomo had his own way of reacting to that indignity. He told Elie to save a tiny bit of the bread that was their daily allotment in the evening and not to eat it until another time. That way, he said, Elie would be in control over a small part of his life at least, even in camp. Elie was too hungry to mind him the first time. Later he came to understand the wisdom of Shlomo's suggestion.

Elie quickly learned that the kapos who guarded the inmates were often more brutal and dangerous than the SS captors in charge of the camp. Kapos were usually political prisoners, former criminals, who received small favors from the prison authorities in exchange for supervising their fellow prisoners. The favors were larger food rations or more lenient treatment. Having sold themselves to the Germans and knowing how hated they were by the camp inmates made the kapos very vicious. They were ever ready to vent their aggressive feelings on their fellow prisoners over whose lives they had overwhelming power. Elie quickly minded Shlomo's advice to remain inconspicuous in order to avoid the wrath of any kapo.

Death was a constant presence. It surrounded the inmates at every moment of the day. Each man knew that his life hinged only on his strength and capability to work. Once the body weakened due to malnutrition or disease the road led directly to the gas chambers which operated night and day.

Several times during that summer the labor squads returned to camp in the evening and were forced to witness an execution. The men were lined up around the grassy plot near their barracks, facing a gallows erected in the center. Each execution seemed intended as an object lesson, a warning to each prisoner that the same punishment awaited anyone who broke camp rules.

Nothing was as hard to witness as a hanging. The inmates were spared no detail of cruelty, not even the final stage when everyone was forced to march past the gallows to observe closely the body dangling at the end of the rope.

Of all the executions Elie had to attend none

touched him as deeply as watching the death of a very handsome young boy whom he recalled as the "Sad Angel" because of his expressive eyes. The boy was the servant of a kapo foreman who had taken a liking to him and treated him as his son. When the kapo was accused of an act of espionage within the camp, blame also fell on the boy.

Because of his light weight the "Sad Angel" did not die easily. He swung back and forth on the rope for a very long time before his ordeal finally ended. Watching the boy's suffering was an extremely emotional episode for every man in camp. Elie never forgot the nightmarish experience.

Despite the inhuman circumstances in the camp, most prisoners tried to retain their human dignity. One of the men had brought along a pair of phylacteries which he had so far managed to keep with him. Every morning at dawn, even before the rest of the men rose for the morning line-up, the owner of the phylacteries and several others stood up in front of a wall inside the barracks and held a little prayer service. While the one man adjusted the phylacteries on his arm, the others joined him in reciting: "Blessed are You, Lord our God, King of the Universe, Who has sanctified us with His commandments and commanded us to wear tefillin." Then, when he arranged the section of the phylacteries on his forehead, the rest blessed that step by reciting: "Blessed be the Name of His glorious Majesty for ever and ever." Only then were the men ready for their morning service.

For Elie this was a painful time. He had stopped

praying since coming to Auschwitz. From early child-hood Elie had felt a special, almost personal connec-tion to the God of Israel in which he had gloried. Now he questioned the justice of a God who allowed the terrible deeds of torture and evil Elie had witnessed since stepping off the train in Auschwitz. Elie felt that his childhood had been stolen from him. He still believed in God but he could no longer praise Him.

After three weeks at Auschwitz, Elie's group was taken on a four-hour march to Buna, a labor camp, where there was work for the prisoners, most of them Hungarians.

Each time camp inmates were moved, they marched in military style. Every morning when the group marched off to work, every night when they returned to camp, prisoners stepped in cadence. Shlomo had never been in the army and so had never learned to march properly. He was always out of step with the rest of the men. When the guards saw Shlomo like that it gave them an excuse for hitting him.

At Buna Elie was assigned to an indoor warehouse job. Shlomo worked close by. Elie was delighted to stay near his father and protect him as much as possi-ble. If Elie's work took him away from the camp site, he was always anxious to return in the evening, pray-ing he would find his father still alive.

One particular kapo was very jealous of Elie's gold-capped front tooth and showed his eagerness to have the gold. This guard was aware of Elie's concern about his father, so he was especially harsh with Shlomo, beating him whenever he saw him out of step.

Elie determined to help his father by teaching him to march. Every single night after roll call he made him practice outside the barracks while there was still daylight. This went on for two weeks. Elie counted as his father marched, much to the delight of other prisoners who thought the exercise highly entertaining. Unfortunately Elie's training did not work. Shlomo was too tired and too discouraged to learn anything new. He could not change his step nor learn to march in cadence.

Finally Elie was forced to give up. Late one evening, in the latrine, he submitted to the kapo's wish. With the aid of a former dentist from Budapest, and a rusty spoon used as an instrument, Elie underwent an act of "dental surgery." Afterward, without a word, he handed his gold tooth to the kapo.

From the bread crumbs left over from their meager rations Elie and his father made chess figures. Every evening after their meal of thin soup, they played chess until daylight faded from their barracks. They needed to keep their minds active and chose to exercise them even during the worst of conditions.

Being together was vitally important to them both. In the midst of the horror that surrounded them, looking out for each other gave them a reason to survive. Having each other was their only reminder that they had once been a family. Sometimes his father spoke of Elie's mother and the girls in an almost dreamlike manner. Perhaps neither one really wanted to visualize what might have happened to them. It hurt too much to dwell on their fate. But most of the time Elie was too tired even to think. All he wanted to do was to sink down on the hard bunk with its wispy thin layer of straw and be allowed to sleep.

One evening the regular roll call took place earlier than usual, and in the work place rather than on the grassy plot in front of the barracks. Beatings in the concentration camp occurred often and were always public events. They took place in the open space in front of the barracks where all the prisoners were made to watch. The person to be punished was spread out face down over a box, and hit a maximum of twenty-five strokes with a leather whip.

When the kapo called out "A-7713," Elie knew what lay ahead. Just days before he had been unfortunate enough to surprise a kapo in the act of having sex with a young Polish girl, a labor force prisoner, and had not run away fast enough. The kapo had recognized him. This now, was Elie's punishment. First the kapo made a speech about prisoners who meddled in other people's business and needed to learn their lesson. Then Elie was held down while the guard counted out the strokes of the whip. He was aware of twenty-three blows to his body, then he fainted. Cold water was thrown on him to revive him for the last two. While he lay on the ground, Elie's main concern was for his father and how much Shlomo must be suffering to see his son in this situation.

In the days before they left Sighet there had always been people who listened to the forbidden war news coming from the BBC radio programs broadcast from

London and shared their information with their friends. And so it was common knowledge that the fighting was not going well for the Germans in the spring of 1944, especially on the Eastern front, where the Russians were pursuing retreating German troops, pushing them back toward Germany.

While camp inmates had no direct information about outside events, rumors always circulated. An almost certain way to learn whether the war was going badly for the Germans was by the way they treated their prisoners. It grew worse whenever the war news was bad. There were rumors galore shortly after Elie and his father arrived in Buna: a huge Allied invasion had occurred in France on June 6. As the summer of 1944 progressed, the hopes and prayers of the camp inmates were with all those American and British soldiers fighting their way across Europe toward them. Would they reach the camps in time? Would any inmates still be alive?

After his job in the warehouse was completed Elie joined another labor squad working outdoors. He carried bricks, spaded the soil, and loaded heavy stones onto freight cars. It was strenuous for a *yeshiva* student to perform such hard physical work in the summer heat, but Elie was happy to be strong enough to do it. Each day spent at labor was a gift of life. He had witnessed a number of executions right before his eyes on the gallows erected in the center of the prison yard. Each one had been carried out as an object lesson to the prisoners, a warning not to infringe camp rules. And from the periodic Selections, when the SS weeded out those men who had grown too weak to work and led them away, he knew too well what would happen if his strength gave out.

Working next to Elie under the broiling sun was an older man also unused to physical labor. Pinhas was the former director of a rabbinical school in Galicia and had spent all his life studying sacred books. Elie was a student who had planned to become a rabbi. Now he became Pinhas's pupil. While performing their menial tasks in the summer heat, teacher and student recited whole portions of Talmud to each other. They tried to recall from memory passages they had once known in the days not long before. The mental exercises helped to wipe out the misery of the present and eased the hunger, exhaustion, and hopelessness contained in each day. For the teacher it was a reason to live just a little longer. For Elie it kept alive Dodye Feig's last words to him: "You are Jewish, your task is to remain Jewish. The rest is up to God."

As the hot summer slowly made way for the first days of autumn, camp routine did not change very much. Talk among the inmates turned to the approaching High Holy Days of 1944. How would they be able to observe the most sacred Jewish season in these surroundings and under these circumstances?

Elie dreaded the coming of Rosh Hashanah and Yom Kippur. They had been days of the greatest spiritual importance to him in previous times, but that was when he still believed that he had a direct link to God and that his prayers were heard and acted on by the Most High. He had devoted his whole life to serving God. Now everything was reversed. God had disappointed him. Elie hated the very thought of the Holy Days.

On the eve of Rosh Hashanah at Buna, close to ten thousand Jews stood in the open assembly area where they congregated only for camp roll calls or for hangings. Inside electrified barbed-wire fencing and surrounded by smirking SS guards and armed soldiers, the voice of a rabbi led them, without the use of prayerbooks, in observing the start of a new year. Elie stood among them, his heart cold and in despair. How could anyone here ask God for a good new year, knowing that every minute of life on earth was begrudged him by men?

6

Buchenwald

A new dilemma arose as Yom Kippur approached. Should they fast and risk weakness and possible death by skipping the daily ration of bread and soup, or should they eat and violate the primary commandment of a Jew's holiest day?

As Kol Nidre night arrived, all the prisoners hurried back from their work details and cleaned themselves up for the service. They had survived the surveillance of an outdoor Rosh Hashanah service, but caution that the SS might use the highest holy day for some action of their own—one of their favorite maneuvers—now made the men decide to hold the service indoors where the guards would not be present. Every barracks conducted the identical service at the same time, using prayers transcribed onto bits of toilet paper by some of the older religious men in camp who knew them by heart.

As Elie stood among his fellow prisoners, his heart was heavy. In all his fifteen years this had been the holiest of days, looked forward to all year. The prayers uttered by the inmates brought back memories of standing next to Dodye Feig in the hasidic synagogue in Sighet. He thought of the strong emotions that had flooded his being at those services. How he had felt himself a special servant of the Almighty. How he had been so convinced that He had chosen to listen to Elie's prayers and grant them. And now?

Elie mouthed the prayers, but they no longer had meaning. He felt betrayed by the God who had been his whole life. Betrayed and disappointed that God could allow the death and destruction of the very people who believed in Him and do *nothing*. Filled with unbearable pain, Elie fell asleep that Kol Nidre, certain that it was the worst night of his life.

Pinhas, his teacher while working in the fields, told Elie that he would not fast. Such a decision from a highly religious man convinced Elie that his teacher, too, had lost his faith. Shlomo also gave him strict orders not to fast. The following day—Yom Kippur— while out on the digging detail, Elie swallowed the thin soup and the dry bread doled out to the prisoners and was amazed that he felt nothing.

Shlomo was getting weaker. Elie, seeing him more depressed and hopeless as the weeks progressed, worried that his father would not pass the next Selection.

And he was right. When the SS once again paraded the naked prisoners in front of the dreaded "Angel of Death," Dr. Mengele, Elie saw his father's name being added to the list. That list meant certain death. Now Elie was petrified. On the day Shlomo and others were due to be taken away, Elie ran back as fast as he could from his work detail to his barracks to make certain whether his father was still there. His heart beat with fear. He reached his bunk and there was Shlomo! Saved once more. It was a miracle.

Pinhas was not so fortunate. The scholar who afterward told Elie that he had fasted after all, not out of conviction but out of defiance, had grown weak and feeble in recent weeks and was condemned to die at Dr. Mengele's last Selection. Elie missed him dreadfully. The older man had kept Elie's mind and heart occupied during their time together. Now hopelessness won out again.

Elie stayed as close as possible to his father in the closing days of autumn. As both grew weaker they did not talk as much as before, but their togetherness still sustained them throughout the chilly days and icy nights and gave them a reason for holding on just a little bit longer.

As 1944 neared its end and the days grew still colder, the prisoners' shirts were exchanged for some a little heavier. The food rations remained the same: black coffee, dry bread, thin soup. It was harder to stand up straight in the icy wind during roll call. Every morning there were more dead bodies in the bunks: prisoners who had frozen to death in the night.

Elie was now working on a brick-moving detail. On several occasions he found that the cold fused his hands to the bricks. One morning in the middle of January 1945 he discovered that his foot had swollen to almost twice its size. The pain was so intense he could not step on it. He had no choice but to have it examined at the camp hospital. There the doctor, formerly a famous Hungarian surgeon, told Elie that the foot needed to be operated on or Elie might lose some of the toes, perhaps even the leg itself. At the thought of a possible amputation Elie again wondered how his father would manage without his help.

The prison hospital was located in one of the barracks and had few instruments and no pain-killing medications. Its only luxury was a cot with a clean white sheet on it. Despite his great fear, Elie liked the doctor instantly and trusted him. Surgery was set for the next day. The doctor told Elie he would have to be brave and bear the pain the best way he could. Sometime during the hour-long procedure Elie fainted.

He awoke, afraid of the worst, but the surgeon assured him he had only drained the foot of infection and that it would heal properly within two weeks. Relieved, Elie fell back on the cot and enjoyed the feel of a clean bed for the first time since he had left Sighet in April.

His recuperation was marred by rumors that Russian troops were advancing faster than expected and would liberate the camp within hours. It seemed the rumors were true: the sound of gunfire had been heard nearby in recent days. Buna would be evacuated within the next few days. All the inmates felt certain the Germans would not leave any of their prisoners behind to fall into Russian hands and have the liberators discover the inhuman condition of the Nazi camps.

Two days later came orders that all prisoners were to be moved to the camp at Buchenwald near the city of Weimar, deep within Germany. Elie, lying in bed while his foot was healing, wondered whether it would not be easier to let the SS kill him here and now than to attempt to march to the next camp.

Although he dreaded the journey ahead, Elie and his father decided to be evacuated from Buna in hopes of saving their lives. Elie's dread became reality on the ten-day walk to Buchenwald that became known as the Death March because so many of the prisoners died enroute to the new camp. The Germans welcomed these losses: fewer prisoners meant less precious food wasted, and possibly fewer accusers if the Allies advanced on them too quickly, for every day it became clearer that Germany was losing the war.

Elie trudged in the snow with bloodied bandages on his throbbing, bleeding foot. No shoe fit over the blanket strips he had ripped up and wrapped over the gauze. Every step was agony and left red droplets on the white snow. All around he saw other marchers collapse in the ice and snow. They were quickly trampled underfoot by the silent, relentless, moving mass of prisoners. Elie saw the SS shoot down any stragglers who could not keep pace. He almost envied them their final rest. They did not have to go on walking.

He hoped that Russian troops would advance and overtake them. The pain and weariness was more than he could bear. Frequently he begged Shlomo to let him sink down into the snow and leave him behind to die. But his father, supportive despite his own terrible fatigue, would not let Elie sink down to sleep. During Elie's worst moments Shlomo was constantly at his side, holding him up and pulling him along. And Elie, in spite of his suffering, knew his father was saving his life.

Somewhere along the way the marchers came to a stop. Although numb in both body and mind, Elie was dimly aware that an old man—Rabbi Eliahou—approached him and asked whether he had seen his son, from whom he had become separated during the march. From the very start of their deportation the aging rabbi from Poland and his son had been part of Elie's group, sharing their fate. Like Shlomo and Elie, Rabbi Eliahou and his son were inseparable and totally devoted to each other. But on the icy walk to Buchenwald the old man became too exhausted to go on and lagged behind.

At that moment Elie was too tired to remember and told the father he had not seen his son. Much later, Elie recalled that he had indeed seen the son. The thought horrified him, for it meant that Rabbi Eliahou's son had realized his father was growing weaker with every step and could not keep up with him. Wishing to rid himself of an unbearable burden, the son had deliberately walked away. Trying to save his own life, he was leaving his father to certain death.

Shocked and terribly saddened, Elie was almost relieved that he had spared the old father the truth. He hoped fervently that he would never be forced into such a choice for himself. Deep in his heart arose a silent prayer that he would never abandon Shlomo the way Rabbi Eliahou's son had abandoned his father.

The last stage of their journey to Buchenwald took place in open boxcars. In space intended for possibly forty men, one hundred stood up leaning against each other. If one man fell, he was in immediate danger of being trampled underfoot. Elie noticed that his father stood with his eyes closed, barely breathing. He did not respond when Elie spoke to him. Elie wondered what would happen if Shlomo died. Then he would no longer have the responsibility to look after his father. He was weary enough to believe that without his father he himself would no longer have to struggle to stay alive. He could give in to his weariness and die too.

At one point the train stopped and the SS men yelled at the prisoners to toss out the dead among them. Some of the stronger men in the boxcar wanted more space for themselves and saw this as their chance. Elie saw two scavengers approach Shlomo, ready to strip off his clothing and throw him out. Yelling hysterically that his father was still alive, Elie hurled himself at the two men and stopped them from taking him. The train went on, leaving behind naked corpses in the snow.

At last the prisoners arrived in Buchenwald, just as an air raid alert took place. In the darkness Elie and

Shlomo became separated. Elie found a wooden plank in a nearby bunk and fell asleep instantly. When he awoke in daylight he fought desperately against the thoughts racing through his brain. What if Shlomo had not lived out the journey? Would it not then be easier for Elie to survive, without constantly worrying about his father? Suddenly Elie knew his thoughts were those Rabbi Eliahou's son had experienced and obeyed. Elie felt a deep, burning shame that he too,was struggling with these thoughts.

When he finally found his father Elie vowed to himself not to let Shlomo out of his sight again, but to stay close to him no matter how difficult that would be.

Shlomo was now so deathly ill from dysentery he could barely stand. Most of the time he lay on the straw of his bunk, his eyes glazed, his lips cracking from high fever. Elie did not eat one of his evening rations of bread, and with it bribed another prisoner to switch places with him so Elie could have the bunk space right above Shlomo. Now he tried to minister to his father during the night and as much of the day that camp routine allowed. But he could see that Shlomo was slipping away. Every day he grew a little worse. Elie was frantic about being away from his father during the daytime, for he knew that not only did the guards hit Shlomo during his absence but other prisoners stole his rations from him.

On the morning of January 29, 1945 Elie awoke to find his father's space empty in the bunk below. He did not know whether Shlomo had actually died in the night or whether he had been removed while still alive. He was never to know the truth. He did know that Shlomo had gone from his life forever. As a pious Jewish son, he did not have the consolation of a burial service. There was no one to comfort him. Nothing could heal his grief. His soul was so frozen with pain he could not even cry.

After his father's death Elie was removed to the children's bunker at Buchenwald. Here about six hundred youngsters aged ten to seventeen were housed. Most of them, like Elie, had lied about their age and because they were strong enough to work had been able to stay with a family member until the relative died. Conditions in the children's compound were somewhat better, mainly because its inmates did not have to work. However, Elie was so distressed and weak that he could barely manage the two daily roll calls and the food line-up for soup and bread. Most of the time he lay in the straw of his bunk feeling too weary to think of anything but food.

As winter turned to spring and British and American forces reached and crossed the Rhine into Germany, coming ever closer, the SS began evacuating Buchenwald. Each day about one thousand prisoners were marched out of its gates. None of them returned. Those still in camp were convinced that they had been shot and dreaded their own turn at "evacuation." There were rumors that as soon as all prisoners had been killed Buchenwald would be burned down by the SS.

On the evening of April 11, 1945, tanks of the U.S.

Third Army arrived at the gates of Buchenwald. American soldiers entered and stared in horror at the twenty thousand living skeletons—among them several hundred children—who greeted them with their

Elie (circled) *and fellow Jews after U.S. troops liberated Buchenwald. (Culver Pictures)*

tears of joy. For the former inmates of the concentration camp freedom had come.

Elie awoke in the U.S. army hospital where he had lain for many days in a deep coma and high fever. While unconscious, he had called out for his mother and believed her to be near, at times even feeling her cool touch on his forehead. When he woke up, lying on clean sheets on an army cot, he was confused. He remembered very little that had happened to him, but he knew he was very ill and might still die. In his feverish state he thought how ironic it would be to die just when he became liberated.

To the medical personnel who had converted the former SS hospital to house the many seriously ill camp inmates, Elie's case was all too clear. He was suffering from food poisoning. When the American troops first entered the camp and saw the starving inmates, they had immediately begun to give them food. Some of the soldiers, feeling guilty at the sight of such acute suffering, even shared their own food rations with the camp survivors. What they did not consider was that, after such a long time of not eating regular meals, the prisoners' digestive systems were not ready to handle normal food. In Elie's case there was an additional twist. During the time the SS had abandoned Buchenwald and the American liberators had entered the camp, he had not eaten for six days. He was so starved that he gobbled up everything the Americans gave him, including a piece of ham. In his whole life as a religious Jew Elie had never eaten pork.

The army nurses who fed him and the military doctors who prescribed medications eventually brought down his fever. Restoring some of his strength took much longer. Elie required two weeks of recuperation before he could be discharged from the army hospital.

An American officer interviewed him and asked Elie whether he had any plans for the future. In his weakness and confusion Elie did not know what to answer. His future? Until now he did not even believe he had a future. Suddenly he had to make a choice and did not know what to do.

"Would you like to go home?" asked the American.

On his table the officer had lists of survivors. He let Elie thumb through them, searching for the names of his mother, his sisters, his grandfather. Nothing. Nothing. Not one member of his family was left. He had lost his whole world.

Elie looked at the kind man sitting opposite him. He was sure the officer meant well. In Elie's mind was a last picture of Sighet on the hot morning he had left it. He again saw the long human snake of Jewish residents moving slowly around the town square on their final journey toward the train station. That Sighet was now *judenrein*, devoid of Jews, just as its inhabitants had wanted it to be.

How could he go home without his mother and Shlomo to receive him, without Dodye Feig to bless him? He had no home to go back to.

7

Freedom

Although the German High
Command had not yet signed the official document of sur-
render, for the four hundred boy survivors aboard the train
that rolled into a smoke-filled Paris train depot on an April
morning in 1945, the war was over. Elie, at sixteen, was one
of the gaunt, weary youngsters who stared at the swarm of
Jewish welfare workers, reporters, and translators who
greeted them. Their once-shaven heads sprouted fresh stiff
stubble. New, ill-fitting clothes replaced the striped camp
garb left behind in Germany.

Escorted by American army personnel, the emaciat-
ed survivors had traveled by train for two days, from
Germany to Belgium, then to France, where the
Americans tried to negotiate admission for their

charges. Finally a special order from General Charles de Gaulle reached the train: they were invited to live in France.

For many of the boys it was a major disappointment not to go to Palestine. That had been their dream during the worst days of their captivity. And now they learned that the British government had closed the door to Palestine, refusing all entrance to Jewish immigrants! Still, the idea of going to Paris sounded exciting, until they realized that no one in the group understood a word of the new language that awaited them. Who among them spoke French, after all?

Elie stood subdued and forlorn in the bustling foreign railroad station. Around him swirled all the people in charge of his future. Most of the other boys munched silently on the food the social workers had given them. But Elie was still unable to digest food without experiencing violent cramping, so he chose not to eat at all.

After hours of listing names and registration formalities the authorities divided the newcomers into two groups: those who observed the Jewish dietary laws and those to whom it did not matter. Elie wanted to stay with the religious group. As a mark of respect to his lost family and because he was the only surviving male, Elie chose to remain faithful to his religious upbringing. It was one of the few traditions left to him.

Finally, the youngsters were placed on yet another train. This time their destination was the town of Ecouis in the province of Normandy, where a former castle had been converted into a vacation home. It was hoped that with good food, sunshine, and rest their bodies would fill out again and their minds would recover from the horrendous ordeals of the recent past.

In Ecouis, in the flower-filled gardens of the former Normandy estate that had once belonged to French aristocracy, Elie and his fellow survivors of Buchenwald's children's block walked, breathed the clean air, and felt miserable, lonely, and lost. As May turned into June of 1945, it became clearer to them with each passing day that a hoped-for reunion with loved ones who might have survived would not occur. The deprived, malnourished children ate and appreciated the good, healthy food prepared for them. The excellent milk and cheeses, the splendid fruit of the Normandy countryside nourished their starving bodies. They attempted to talk to the social workers who tried hard to ease their concerns, but nothing erased their grief and suffering.

The youngsters, aged ten through seventeen, huddled together, having only each other for company. None of them spoke or understood French. Unheard-of worlds lay between them and their new hosts. Hate had orphaned them. It had stolen their families, their homes, their childhood. How could anyone understand how they felt? Their lives had been dashed to pieces, but, to their suprise, they had survived. Now most of them did not know what to do with the lives that had been given back to them.

Elie spent much time out-of-doors in the radiant

Normandy sunshine. On his solitary walks in the pleasant spring temperatures he tried to thaw the eternal cold in his bones while he thought about his future. What would he do? How would he live? How could he even function in a new land and a new language? At home in Sighet he had considered becoming a rabbi or a teacher. But now? What should he do first?

His religious training had taught him that it is the role of a survivor to testify about what he has seen. His testimony must serve as a warning. No one should ever again have to experience what he had suffered. But how could he tell his story without the proper skills? He was certainly not ready to deal with his memories nor to describe what he had seen.

Elie decided on a vow of silence. He would wait, as long as ten years, if necessary, before giving the testimony his experiences required. In his lost adolescence he had dreamed of writing religious books. Now he knew his writing would have to describe a world far removed from religion.

One of the greatest gifts Shlomo had given him was the desire for study. His father had believed study would supply answers to most of the world's problems. Through study Elie hoped to find meaning in his fate and the fates of all those he had loved. Why had it happened? For the Event (what else could anyone call it?) was so incomprehensible that one could not even speak of it. What words were there for the unspeakable?

If writing was to be his method of transmitting what he had lived through, he had to learn and polish the skills for such a task. He would study languages, he would study history, he would study psychology. Study was the key word. It would be his goal until that far-off day when he would be ready to abandon the self-imposed vow of silence to tell his story. For the first time since leaving Sighet, Elie felt there might be a reason for having survived.

Now that he had convinced himself to continue with his interrupted education, Elie asked for an interview with the head of the children's home to request the use of some books necessary to his Talmud studies. When he walked into the director's room he found the man talking on the telephone. It seemed to Elie that he heard his name mentioned, but since Monsieur Wolff spoke in French and Elie did not understand the rest of the conversation, he sat down quietly to wait until the director was finished. Just then Monsieur Wolff hung up the telephone, turned to Elie, and said: "That was your sister calling from Paris."

Elie was stunned. He tried to convince the director that there must be an error. Elie had no reason to believe that any of his family members had survived. He had looked through the many lists of survivors that were shown him in Germany and had found no one related to him on them. He had assumed that all his relatives had perished.

The director listened patiently. He nodded his head in agreement when Elie gave him his reasons for doubting the news. Then Monsieur Wolff told him what he had learned. The story was indeed amazing.

It affirmed to Elie the ancient Jewish belief that nothing in life is an accident, but an event ordained to happen.

A young woman, newly married to a fellow survivor, also liberated from Auschwitz like her, had emigrated to France with her husband. Her French was not very good, but she was trying to improve it by reading the daily newspapers. One night she picked up the Paris newspaper and read about a group of Jewish children freed from Buchenwald who had just arrived in France and had been sent to a rest home in Normandy to recuperate. Pointing to a photograph in the article, she was overcome with emotion and screamed, "That's Leizer!"

As quickly as they could, the young couple went to the nearest post office, purchased the necessary token for a long-distance call, and contacted the children's home in Ecouis. There Monsieur Wolff was happy to confirm to Hilda the good news that her brother Leizer was indeed one of his charges. He arranged to send Elie to Paris for a reunion with her the following day.

Elie had trouble sleeping that night. He still did not believe that his sister was alive and feared that great disappointment lay ahead if the wrong person met the train in Paris. But it was really his older sister Hilda who was waiting for him at the Gare Saint-Lazare, laughing and crying as she held out her arms to enfold him. And the story she had to tell was truly miraculous.

Both she and the middle sister, Bea, had survived

Auschwitz and, while still in camp, had learned that their mother and little sister had died there very soon after their arrival. When Hilda and her new husband went to Paris, Bea decided to return to Sighet to search for Elie. In Sighet she was told by other returnees that Elie too, had perished in the camps. Filled with great sadness, she had reported the news to Hilda. Bea then made plans for her own eventual emigration to Canada. In Paris one evening Hilda had opened the newspaper and had seen the article and Elie's picture.

After only one day in Paris, Elie returned to the children's home in Normandy. It was a painful decision for him and his sister to separate again, but Hilda and her husband were very poor and lived in a one-room flat, with barely enough money for food. Elie, on the other hand, was being supported by the children's agency, the OSE (Oeuvre de Secours aux Enfants), who had placed him and the other surviving boys in their Normandy estate. It was the only possible solution for the moment, but when amid general sadness Elie climbed aboard the evening train he at least knew that his sisters were alive and that at some point in the future they would all meet again.

8

Paris

After the first four weeks in France, Elie was moved from Normandy to another chateau near the town of Amblois, closer to Paris. There he began studying French in earnest. He listened closely to staff and visitors, tried to read whatever written material was available, and carried a small pocket dictionary to look up every unfamiliar word.

He moved even closer to Paris when he was transferred to yet another chateau, this one near the town of Taverny. There was a sizable group of religious youngsters at Taverny who encouraged each other in their studies. Elie, who at sixteen was one of the older youngsters, even began teaching a few of the younger boys Hebrew.

As the summer progressed he made up his mind to learn French well enough to attend the Sorbonne, the University of Paris, and study philosophy. He hoped this would help him to understand himself and the world around him. When he was moved once again, this time to a chateau in Versailles, only forty minutes from Paris, he knew he was heading closer to his goal. Soon he would be living in the capital city.

While at Versailles Elie met a young man who understood his eagerness to get to Paris. François Wahl was already a graduate student in philosophy at the Sorbonne. When he learned that some young people who had survived the concentration camps were housed at the nearby chateau, he walked into the building one day and offered to help in any way he could. Someone introduced him to Elie.

François became Elie's first French teacher. He came to the chateau several times a week and brought books that introduced Elie to French culture at the same time he was learning the language. For Elie it became a summer of discovery. He found himself starting anew. Not only had France become his new home, a shelter from his unhappy recent past, but he was entering a new world. He tried to think of it as a new beginning.

As summer turned into fall of 1945, Elie knew that his weeks at the Versailles chateau would soon end. The agency announced that it was disbanding the group. Most of the boys with whom he had come to France would scatter in all directions. Elie had chosen to go to Paris. There he would have to live and work on his own.

Life in the city of Paris meant a tiny room in a poor working-class tenement in the Marais, the Jewish Quarter. Here a bed, a chair, and a small table constituted Elie's world when at the end of September he turned eighteen. A small scholarship from the OSE paid for his room rent and one meal a day at a local bistro. As a foreigner he was not allowed a work permit.

Elie was often hungry. When he dreamed of luxury it meant an unattainable extra cup of coffee with real milk at the bistro. More painful than hunger, however, was the enormous grief he carried inside. He spoke to no one and few people spoke to him. His landlady and fellow tenants avoided the skinny, silent young man with the sad eyes. He did not see even his sister very often. She and her husband were so poor they just managed to survive from day to day. And for Elie even the fare on the Metro to their flat was a luxury.

During many sleepless nights Elie wished that he had died along with his dear ones. The pain of surviving was so great that he envied the dead for not having to struggle any longer. He felt guilty that he might be alive at the expense of another, far worthier life. And, like many other survivors, he questioned why he was spared. What was his purpose in life? What was his mission?

Restlessness drove him on long walks of exploration throughout Paris. He covered its various neighborhoods in depth. He strolled along both sides of the River Seine and discovered the booksellers whose wares he was too poor to buy. He visited and studied the magnificent art in the great museums of Paris. When he became tired of walking, he sat on park benches and read or studied the passersby.

He tried to push away the thoughts of his lost family that were constantly on his mind. Soon another worry invaded his thoughts. The agency had informed him that it would stop its payments to him. Any day now his money would run out. How would he live? He did not need much food, but what about the rent?

One night he entered one of several synagogues he had discovered during his rambles through the area of the Jewish district. He had learned that many refugees attended this particular synagogue. When he saw how sparse was the number of worshippers, he recalled Dodye Feig and the joyful congregation at the hasidic synagogue in Sighet. Pain shot through him as he observed the disinterested men who spoke to each other of politics, high prices, and world events during the service.

Afterward he approached one of the men and inquired about the chances of finding work. He would do any job, he told the congregant. He was starving. He needed work, any work, to live. In reply he received a lecture about the current poor economic situation in France and how many foreigners took away work from Frenchmen who needed jobs. Elie was mortified at such a reaction. Finally, however, the man felt moved to direct Elie to a relief agency that could possibly help him.

When he visited this agency a few days later Elie underwent a humiliating three-hour questioning that left him so angry and deflated he wished he had the strength to yell at the agency worker and cause a disturbance in the office. But the important thing was the handful of French francs with which he left that day—enough to pay the landlady for several weeks ahead. Even more important, he had a few bills left over. Clutching them, he crossed one of the bridges to the Left Bank of Paris, headed straight toward the university district and the buildings of the Sorbonne, and registered as a student.

Along with his great desire for learning, a new consideration had entered Elie's life. He had discovered that as a student he was eligible for a work permit in France. For the first time in his life he could not honestly decide which was the more important: to study or to work.

The lean, intense young man with a strong foreign accent took his learning seriously. He sat in the huge, ancient lecture halls of the Sorbonne in the Latin Quarter of Paris and absorbed every word as if his life hinged on it. For Elie believed that study was his road back to the world of the living after his trip to hell. He enrolled in courses to help him along that road: philosophy, psychology, and literature. Literature was a special revelation to him: for the first time he read novels and stories just for pleasure. In Sighet all his reading had been devoted to religious texts and their analysis. Now he found whole new worlds opening up to him.

In the cafes on the rue St. Germain-des-Prés near the university, modern thinkers like Sartre, de

Beauvoir, and Camus met to discuss the enormous tragedies that had befallen Europe and its people during World War II. These postwar philosophers were extremely popular with students, who gathered near them hoping to overhear some of their conversation. Elie too, read the writings of the thinkers of the day and was influenced by them. He especially liked the writings of Albert Camus, whose words touched him deeply. They seemed to speak to him personally. Camus wrote about a world that had been turned upside down leaving few values intact. Except for friendship. The commitment of people toward each other still existed. Despite the enormous hurt inside him, Elie could share that opinion. He could even agree that friendship made living worthwhile.

On a few occasions Elie looked longingly through the windows of one of the famous cafes because he thought he glimpsed Albert Camus inside. Not having money for the cup of coffee that would have allowed him admission, Elie walked on.

He had neither time nor funds to participate in the diversions and pleasures that were part of Parisian student life. He was far too serious to spend time on drink or parties. When he did not study, he worked. He accepted every job that came his way. The few francs he earned kept him alive. He worked as tutor, translator, choir director, and camp counselor. Employment agencies sent him to the homes of wealthy French Jews who needed a teacher for their children, but he was unhappy with his students because they were not interested in studying, and they in turn thought him too intense and demanding a teacher. Paralyzed by grief and loneliness, he shut himself up tightly against everything new.

From time to time Elie attended worship services at a small neighborhood synagogue in the rue Pave. There one Friday night he noticed a strange, old man whom he had not seen before. The stranger's appearance and behavior disturbed Elie. He was unkempt and dressed like a vagabond, wearing a hat much too small for his large, round head and thick eyeglasses too smudged for him to see through. His voice was harsh and aggressive as he stood in the midst of a group of worshippers and explained the meaning of the day's Torah portion to them after the service had ended. Elie was annoyed by the man's slovenly appearance and his arrogant manner, but one thing was clear to him. He had never heard anyone speak so brilliantly and illuminatingly before. Right then Elie knew that no matter how unappealing the person was to him, he must become this man's student.

That evening did not end well for such a project. The old man had noticed Elie too, and drew him into conversation. But Elie's words, meant to compliment, infuriated the man. Instead of replying to Elie, he turned and ran off, visibly angry. Elie was shocked; he had meant well. Others in the synagogue tried to console him. They told him the old man's behavior was always odd. This evening had been no different from many others. But their words did not ease his distress.

Elie walked the Paris streets for a long time that night, wondering what he had said to annoy the man.

He knew he had to find him again. No one at the synagogue knew his name or where he lived. But as he returned to his poor little room, discouraged and alone, Elie realized that for the first time since the horror of the camps he was interested in something again. Not since his masters in Sighet had anyone so stimulated and excited his brain as had the eccentric man whose dazzling explanations he had heard this evening. They had to become teacher and student. It was fated, he knew.

Elie had to wait for quite some time before he met him again, for the strange old man did not return to the synagogue. Weeks later, on a train to a Paris suburb where Elie taught Talmud to a group of hasidic refugee students, he heard someone call out to him, turned around, and saw the mysterious stranger again.

When they got off the train, the old man followed Elie to the chateau where his students lived and, as if fate had planned it that way, took over the scheduled lecture with one of his own. It was the most amazing session Elie had ever heard. The stranger hypnotized both Elie and his students with his knowledge. He took bits of information from the religious text, mixed them with items of current events and questions the students asked, and wove them together into one harmonizing speech.

Day turned into night, yet no one rose to leave. The single lesson Elie had prepared was replaced by a whole week of the old man's teaching. He was so stunningly brilliant that Elie did not mind in the least that he was no longer the teacher.

During the next three years, from late in 1945 until the end of 1948, his visitor walked upstairs twice every week to Elie's tiny, shabby room in the Jewish Quarter of Paris. Elie never knew at just what hour to expect his teacher, for night and day were as unimportant to the old man's schedule as were his needs for food and sleep.

While his Master sat in the room's only chair, Elie sat on his bed and listened to the old man talk about language, philosophy, religion, his every statement embroidered with such vast amounts of knowledge that Elie found it nearly incredible. He had never expected to learn so much from only one teacher.

The old man revealed nothing about himself or his background, and grew noticeably angry when asked any questions. Elie did not even know his name. Many, many years later, after his teacher had died, Elie received a letter from a man who claimed to have been a close relative. From him Elie found out that his Master's name had been Mordecai Shushani, that he had mastered thirty languages, had memorized the Book of Splendor and various sacred writings of other religions, and had been acquainted with almost every culture that had ever existed on earth.

In May 1948, while Elie was still studying with the old man, the State of Israel came into being. His teacher discussed the birth of the new nation with him one night at the same small synagogue where they had first met. Elie had gone to Friday night services excited and happy. To him, who had lost everything—his past, his world, his identity—the establishment of Israel was nothing less than a miracle. As he says, "Overnight I was robbed of even the smallest point of reference and support. I was confronted with emptiness. Everywhere. To avoid sinking, I needed a miracle, or at least a sign."

But his teacher disagreed. "Call it miraculous, that I refuse. We have paid too dearly for it. To be a miracle, it would have had to happen a little sooner."

As soon as the new State of Israel was born, it was attacked by its neighbors who begrudged its existence and forced it to fight. Immediately after he heard that war had broken out, Elie rushed to the Israeli recruiting office in Paris and volunteered to fight. But the concentration camp experience had left him frail and underweight, and to his regret he was turned down.

Toward the end of 1948, his Master disappeared from Elie's life just as mysteriously as he had entered it. One night Elie walked the old man to the Metro stop, as he did after every lesson, and bid him goodbye. He did not know it would be the last time he was to see him. Rav Shushani never came to Elie's room again.

While he was studying at the Sorbonne and having his twice-weekly visits with Rav Shushani, Elie had kept so busy that he had forgotten his loneliness. With the end of the university courses and his Master's departure, that feeling of sadness came back. However, something important had happened to him and he recognized it himself. The lively discussions with Rav Shushani and the huge fund of new knowledge he had received from him had opened Elie up to new ideas and impressions and had changed his life.

Afterward Elie realized that certain events in a person's life occur precisely for a reason. He became convinced that meeting the mysterious stranger had not been an accident but an encounter fated to happen. And that this particular encounter had helped him to bridge the road from death to life.

Anxious to establish a connection between himself and the new Jewish homeland, Elie landed a job as the Paris reporter for the Israeli newspaper *Yedioth Ahronot*. Having a press card meant travel, for air and ship lines gave free passage to reporters. Restless and lonesome as he was, Elie availed himself of every possible writing assignment that might take him to new locations. He had no one waiting for him in Paris, his sisters did not need him, and the questions that troubled him still waited for answers. He thought often of his father who had insisted that Elie learn to speak and write *Ivrit*, modern Hebrew. Now Elie had to write his articles in that language. He was frequently grateful to Shlomo for pushing him to learn foreign languages and often wished he could tell him so.

9

An Interview Unlike Any Other

Elie's press card became his passport to countries and cities all over the world. As soon as his newspaper cabled him an assignment, he was off to yet another new site to gather material and write his story. Restless and lonely, he traveled as far as South America and North Africa, and to exotic and strange countries like India. He welcomed the chance to discover new places. Perhaps he hoped to forget the one town that was lost to him, his hometown Sighet. Next to Sighet, only one other place on earth drew him. That place was Jerusalem, and he longed for it.

The first time he received an assignment to visit Israel was early in 1949. He wandered through the ancient streets of Jerusalem seeking the vision he had dreamed of as a child when his parents' Passover seder concluded with the wish, "Next year in Jerusalem."

But the City of Peace was not wearing her normal face. Her streets were filled with young soldiers, guns, barbed wire, and explosions. He stayed only briefly that first time, hoping that when he returned for future visits tranquility and harmony might reside in the land of Israel.

In 1952 he was sent to the Netherlands. In the town of Wassenaar, a suburb of the Hague, Elie covered the first postwar Israeli-German conference on the reparations Germany would pay into the treasury of the State of Israel on behalf of the victims of Nazi brutality. It was a difficult assignment for him. Hearing how "blood money" was negotiated in payment for lost lives and property caused him personal pain. After the talks ended, the head of the German negotiating team walked to the press table to thank the reporters who had covered the event. All but one of the correspondents responded to the negotiator. Elie looked straight past him. Shake hands with a German? It was something he found impossible to do.

Two years later, in 1954, another "encounter" took place which would give Elie's life a new direction. He had arranged to interview a famous French Catholic writer and philosopher, François Mauriac, winner of the 1952 Nobel Prize for Literature. In the man's Paris apartment Elie grew increasingly irritated by Mauriac's comments regarding his love of the Jewish people, especially, however, for the Jew Jesus, who had given his life for his people whom he could not save, but who had saved mankind instead.

Suddenly Elie closed his notebook and stood up. "You speak of Christ, sir," he said, "of his suffering, of his death. Christian people like to speak of Christ. But I want you to know that ten years ago not very far from here I knew Jewish children who suffered and died in ways a thousand times worse than Christ on the cross. And we don't speak of them."

Totally contrary to his usual polite demeanor, Elie then ran out of the apartment. While he stood waiting for the elevator, Mauriac, who had followed Elie outside, pulled on his sleeve and asked him to come back inside. In the drawing room, sitting across from Elie, the old man wept at the story of Elie's torment. Elie, mortified over his unprofessional, tactless behavior, wished he could disappear into thin air.

Mauriac would not let him apologize. He asked Elie questions, questions about the very topic on which Elie had vowed to keep silent. Gently, tenderly, the old writer prompted him to speak of everything—the sealed trains, the camps, death, loss, ... and the terrible, relentless, inhuman brutality he had experienced. Elie answered all the questions with the barest of words. Finally he burst out that he couldn't speak of these things, that he had taken a vow of silence not to reveal them.

When after several hours the interview ended, Mauriac had convinced the twenty-six-year-old reporter that he must no longer remain silent, that it was even wrong to do so. As he escorted Elie to the elevator he again urged Elie to write down everything he had never mentioned to another living being. All of it. It was his duty as a witness, Mauriac reminded him.

The reporting assignment Elie felt he had so mishandled left him strangely relieved and at ease. The words of the famous writer melted some of the ice of grief within Elie's heart. They gave him, a poor, young, stateless Jewish refugee, a feeling that he mattered, that what he had to say should be heard, in fact, must be heard.

It was during 1954, the tenth year since he had taken the vow of silence, that Elie sat down to write. For the next twelve months he sat in his room at night and wrote by hand and in Yiddish. He recorded every step of the journey he and his family had taken from the spring day in 1944 when they left Sighet until April 11, 1945 when he was liberated from Buchenwald by American soldiers.

It became a manuscript of over eight hundred pages. Elie named it "And the World Stayed Silent" and sent it to a Yiddish press in Argentina, which published it in 1954. He was totally unsuccessful in finding a French publisher, however. No one there was interested in printing it. Finally Elie himself cut the manuscript down to a slim 160 pages and translated it into French. When he was satisfied with the result, he gave his work the name "La Nuit" (Night) and dedicated it to the memory of his parents and his little sister, Tsiporah.

He took the finished manuscript to François Mauriac, who wrote a foreword for it. Then Mauriac gave the book to his own publisher and asked him to print it. The man who had released Elie from his vow of silence and had helped him find his "voice" remained his lifelong friend. The book, *Night*, began its journey around the world.

10

An Act of Fate

In 1956, even before *Night* appeared in Paris, Elie flew to New York to work as a United Nations correspondent for his Israeli newspaper, *Yedioth Ahronot*. He enjoyed New York, its restless energy, its creative drive. He knew very few people, which gave him a chance to spend almost all his time concentrating on his work.

He began each morning at his portable typewriter in his narrow, dark room on 103rd Street on Manhattan's West Side, working from six to ten o'clock before he even commuted crosstown to his jobs. He spent several hours daily in the UN's glittering steel-and-green glass complex of buildings near the East River. He knew almost no one there and spoke very little. His fellow-reporters at the UN took the solitary, pale, dark-haired young man to be an Israeli. Elie sat quietly in a glass chamber and listened through earphones to the French version of the multi-lingual UN sessions. After gathering pertinent information he cabled his articles to his editor in Jerusalem, where news of the United Nations was then of great interest.

In the afternoon he walked through the bustling, crowded lower East Side streets to the *Jewish Daily Forward* building, an important Yiddish newspaper. He earned $175 a month there, working in the editorial department as copy editor and translator and writing current-events pieces for the large Jewish-American readership that liked its news in Yiddish.

Meanwhile he tried to find an American publisher who might bring *Night* to English-reading readers. His friend Georges Borchard, whom he knew from France and was now a Manhattan literary agent, contacted every major New York publishing house in hopes of selling the book, now in English translation. The results were discouraging. On Elie's writing table the rejection slips piled up. They praised his beautiful writing but hinted that his subject matter was too upsetting for American readers.

He brooded over those comments. In writing *Night* he had concentrated on the story of one family, his own, in its fatal voyage through the hell of Nazi concentration camps. With very simple words he had tried to portray the destiny of his dear ones caught in a world of total hate. Until Elie coined the word

"Holocaust" to describe these unspeakable events, that term had not yet been used. It broke his heart to know that six million people had died while the world turned its back on their memory, not even wishing to hear about their fate.

After *Night* had been turned down by dozens of American publishers, it reached the eyes of Arthur Wang, a partner in the New York publishing house of Hill and Wang. Mr. Wang was extremely moved by the translated manuscript and decided to take a chance on the unknown young writer. *Night* was bought by Hill and Wang in July 1959. Elie received an advance of one hundred dollars. Eighteen months after its publication only 1,046 copies had been sold.

But the self-imposed seal of silence had finally been broken. Now a torrent of thoughts and ideas tumbled out of him and drove him to put them on paper. He still felt guilty to have survived while so many others had not. He saw his testimony as the price of being alive. The best way he could testify was to write.

He was already working on a second book. It was to be the story of a young concentration camp survivor who has been assigned to kill a British officer in reprisal for the scheduled execution at dawn of a young Jewish terrorist sentenced by the British occupation forces.

On a stifling hot Sunday afternoon in his first New York July, Elie was on his way to an air-conditioned movie. He stepped off a curb trying to cross the busy intersection at Times Square, and a speeding taxi hit him. With several crushed bones, in overwhelming pain, he lay bleeding in the street. He was aware of being put on a stretcher. Before he lost consciousness, he thought he heard the ambulance helper say, "This one will never make it." Then sirens blared and darkness blotted out his memory.

For many days Elie's life hung on a thread. Even after he knew he would recover, it took seven months of hospitalization for his broken bones to mend. It was a difficult, lonely time.

It took even longer after the seven months in the hospital for Elie to recuperate from the accident. For many months he was housebound and forced to use a wheelchair. Traveling to his two daily jobs became impossible. Using his accident as inspiration, he started to work on his third book, *Le Jour*, which was later translated as *The Accident*.

In the meantime, however, he was very concerned about his French travel visa, which had been issued for one year and would soon expire. Several exhausting visits by wheelchair and taxi to the U.S. Immigration Office in downtown Manhattan and to the French consulate in mid-town produced no extension of his visitor's visa. The French consular officer, amid shoulder shrugs and upturned palms, declared he could not help, that Elie had to return to Paris to get his papers in order. Elie returned once more to the U.S. Immigration Service, where the official said to him, "There is a way to solve this, you know. Why don't you become an American citizen?"

France had offered him only shelter. Now for the first time in his life someone had offered him a home. Was it another act of fate? Perhaps. Elie accepted the offer with gratitude and in 1958 filed for his First Papers. A year later he became eligible to file for American citizenship, which was granted him in 1963.

11

A Pilgrimage
to the Past

In 1961 Elie covered the trial of Adolf Eichmann for his old Israeli newspaper, *Yedioth Ahronot*. He sat in a Jerusalem courtroom during the long trial, which lasted from April 11 until December 15, 1961, and listened to the testimony brought against the Nazi killer who had implemented the Final Solution. This was the name the Germans used when they planned the destruction of the entire Jewish population of Europe.

Adolf Eichmann stood accused of organizing the systematic transportation of every single Jewish community brought to the death camps.

Every single day Elie stared at the prisoner, who was seated in a bullet-proof glass cage. Eichmann wore earphones that translated into German the Hebrew proceedings of the tribunal.

Somewhere deeply embedded in Elie's memory was a picture. He was back at the railroad station in Sighet. The cattle cars had been loaded. The doors were firmly sealed. Through a tiny crack a young boy saw several SS officers in their black uniforms and high shiny boots striding up and down the platform. They were smiling. One of the officers was Colonel Adolf Eichmann, who had come to Sighet to supervise his "project." Elie had not forgotten the face. He was looking at it now when he stared at the prisoner in the glass cage.

What does a killer look like? Do his features resemble those of a grotesque monster? Does his face reveal the evil of his soul? Elie asked himself these questions. But every day after entering the courtroom, he was struck anew by the same thought. How ordinary, how drab and dull was this instrument of mass murder. How hard to reconcile this heinous killer, once the companion and accomplice of Nazi leaders, with the prisoner who pleaded for his life by reciting the boring facts and figures of his inhumane crimes as if they were part of a company report.

In May 1962 Adolf Eichmann was sentenced to death by the Israeli Supreme Court. He was hanged in Tel Aviv on May 31, 1962. Elie found no fault with the verdict. Still, he left the courtroom feeling dissatisfied. He couldn't fathom that a whole race of people could have been so tragically destroyed by a group of men as mediocre and inferior as the man whose trial he had recorded all these days. It was a discovery bitter to accept, especially when Elie contemplated his personal losses.

He had seen his own mother walking away into the flaming Auschwitz night, holding his little sister Tsiporah by the hand, never to return. He had been there to see his father give up his life during a freezing winter in Buchenwald. He had had no exact knowledge of his grandfather's fate until an unsuspecting friend in France presented Elie with a book.

It was a volume of photographs and text, a pictorial history of some of Poland's Jews during the Holocaust, published by the government of postwar Poland in the early 1960s. It was an agonizing experience for Elie to leaf through the pages, like walking through a cemetery filled with loved ones who did not deserve to die. And suddenly he saw a picture that stopped his heartbeat. It was a full-length photograph of an old man standing in a grove of trees, surrounded by laughing German soldiers who were using their daggers to cut off his white beard. Elie recognized the old man at once: it was his grandfather, Dodye Feig. With terrible pain Elie knew he was seeing his grandfather during the last hour of his life. Elie saw the dim outline of people and forest in the photograph's background and it took little imagination to guess what had happened next.

Since his liberation from Buchenwald in 1945, Elie had at times wrestled with the question of his hatred. He had felt then that after all that had happened he would never again be able to feel normally about anything German. He feared that he would hate forever:

its country, its people, even its language. He never believed it possible that he would ever want to visit Germany. But two years after the Eichmann trial he decided to test both himself and postwar Germany. Without a journalistic assignment he flew to Munich. He had scheduled a radio appearance for himself and an evening of readings from his book, *Night*. To his surprise, he found Germany and the people he met there totally different from what he had expected. He thought he would find a nation searching its conscience, but he could discern no noticeable trace of guilt or remorse. Instead of a country trying to recover from the ravages of a war it had lost, Germany was at the peak of international trade, commerce, and the arts. At his Munich reading a young man came to speak to him afterward. "I heard you read tonight, but I must confess concentration camp literature leaves me cold. I just don't understand it."

Elie left after only two days in Germany. He had learned two things of importance to him. The first discovery was that the German people felt neither fear nor shame for what had happened. The memory of the Holocaust lingered with the victims, not with the nation that had inflicted it. The second thing Elie realized was that he could not hate. The strong feelings he had carried inside himself no longer existed. If there was hate, it had evaporated, just as Germany's memory had. In Germany there was nothing left to hate. All that was left in him was sadness.

In the autumn of 1964 Elie decided to return to Sighet for the first time. Twenty years had passed since that sunny summer day when the whole Jewish population had walked to the railroad station on its one-way journey. For Elie it was a visit he both dreaded and longed for. Like a permanent nightmare, the memory of the town had stayed with him during the many years of his wandering. It had found its way into his writing: "It sometimes seems to me that ever since I left it, I have been spending all my time telling about this town which gave me everything and then took it all away" *(The Town Beyond the Wall).*

In his fantasies Elie remembered the hometown of his youth. He saw again the people he had known, the shopkeepers, the teachers, the housewives, hurrying through familiar narrow lanes. He heard the voices of the school masters drilling their students in the *aleph bet* and the joyous singing of Dodye Feig on the Sabbath. He smelled the familiar aromas of the marketplace and of his mother's fragrant warm kitchen at holiday time. He had recorded these memories in stories and novels where they were alive, vivid, and warm.

But there was the dreaded nightmarish side of his memories. In it he saw himself return to Sighet—alone. In his imagination he walked through the familiar streets and saw no one he knew. He saw himself approach the little house of his childhood, push open the squeaking gate into the garden, and walk into an empty landscape. No one replied to his call of greeting. No one was there. And he knew he "would go mad with loneliness."

Elie arrived in Sighet late on a fall night in 1964, in

a taxi that drove him over the surrounding mountains. He checked into a hotel that to him as a youngster had seemed the epitome of luxury, but on his return appeared shabby and run down. When he walked the streets of the town after midnight, he found all the landmarks just as he remembered them. He approached the spot that had drawn him to return to the town: the house of his childhood. He stood by the garden gate, feeling the wind rustling through trees grown tall during his absence, tormented by thoughts. He stepped into the small garden behind the house and peeked into the kitchen window. In the dimness he made out a dangling cross in the spot where a photo of a hasidic leader had once hung. He found the spot where he had buried his Bar Mitzvah watch and dug it up easily. It was "covered with dirt and rust, crawling with worms, unrecognizable, revolting." Finally a barking dog drove him away. He fled back to the town square and spent the rest of the night sleepless on a park bench.

No one recognized him when he walked through familiar streets the following morning. He noticed that "Jews' Street" had been renamed "Street of the Deported." He wandered over to the house of his parents one last time just as its new owner stepped out of the door. Elie wanted to say something to him, but thought better of it. What purpose would it have served? It was as if he had never lived there.

Twenty-four hours after his arrival in Sighet Elie left town again. For him it had been "a journey into nothingness," the final end to his childhood.

12

The Jews
of Silence

The Gates of the Forest
and *The Town Beyond the Wall*, novels that followed
Dawn and *The Accident*, increased Elie's readership
in France, Israel, and the United States. They also
earned him several honors. In 1964 he received the
Prix Rivarol in France and the National Jewish Book
Award in the United States. These were the first of
innumerable awards and prizes bestowed on him.

Early in the 1960s Elie met a remarkable woman
who would have a positive influence on his career.
Lily Edelman was the director of Adult Jewish
Education for B'nai B'rith and the head of that organization's Lecture Bureau. Elie's connection to her
resulted in a close friendship. It also marked a turning
point for him. When Lily Edelman championed him as

a new talent to her associates and booked him for several speaking dates, yet another facet of his career began. He became a public speaker.

From the very beginning Elie's speaking engagements drew full houses. The soft-spoken young man with the strong European accent and dark, melancholy eyes became a magnet for audiences. His mysterious air of sadness and the segments of personal history he allowed them to share appealed to the consciences of his listeners. Elie used these lectures as a means of speaking out on Jewish and world concerns. He gently chided his audiences for their past and present apathy and reminded them that the future of Judaism and the world lay in their hands. Through personal appearances he was able to reach thousands of people. To them he was a witness.

Elie still uses hasidic tales and legends to introduce his message to his audiences. When he lectures he frequently feels he is re-creating the role of the story-teller-preachers of his childhood, the traveling *maggidim*, whose Saturday afternoon sessions in Sighet he tried never to miss. But now he knows that he has indeed become a full-fledged *maggid* in his own right.

The novel *The Gates of the Forest* tells the story of a mysterious messenger of fate, Gavriel, a spirit who moves from the past to the present. During his encounters in the book with several survivors, Gavriel assists them in overcoming the losses of their past. He helps the survivors to give up their dead to the peace they deserve and enables them to return to the world of the living with regained faith.

The writing in *The Gates of the Forest* seemed to reflect Elie's own emotions. His extreme sadness and sense of loss was ever so slowly replaced by a wish to return to life. His great guilt over surviving was changing into a feeling that he was spared for a purpose. What that purpose was he was yet to discover, but in the meantime he knew that he dared not waste a moment of his time on earth.

By 1964 Elie's books began to sell well and he no longer needed to work as a daily reporter to earn his living. He was finally able to concentrate on the full-time writing of books.

It had long been his wish to travel to the Soviet Union. He, like many others, had heard rumors that Jews were persecuted by the Communist government. He wanted to see for himself what had happened to the remnant of the Jewish community in the years since the Germans slaughtered most of it. He wanted to know the truth: did Jews want to continue practicing Judaism or were they prevented from doing so?

During the High Holy Days of 1965 he visited the USSR for the first time, assigned by the *Saturday Evening Post* to write a series of articles about Jews living in postwar Russia. "I went to Russia drawn by the silence of its Jews. I brought back their cry," Elie wrote in the introduction to *The Jews of Silence*, a collection of the articles he wrote after his first trip to the Soviet Union.

Shortly after he arrived in Moscow a stranger approached him and asked in Yiddish, "Do you know what is happening here?" The man disappeared into the crowd before Elie could speak to him. Others touched his arm or winked at him, letting him know they knew he was Jewish. Similar things occurred in every town he visited. He found notes, pieces of paper, in his pocket and suspected that the anonymous writers were afraid to reveal themselves. Elie asked himself, "Why?" Why were they so afraid? Was it that they were not allowed to speak to foreigners? Or did they fear imprisonment for communicating with fellow Jews?

Sometimes he was able to shake off the official guides and hosts who were almost always at his side. He was anxious to talk to ordinary people who could tell him the cause of their terror. "Do not forget us. Tell it all to the outside world," seemed to be the essence of the message the Jews he met tried to convey to him.

One day during Sukkot services in a synagogue in Kiev, Elie heard bits and pieces of Hebrew that did not belong to the prayers just then recited. The voice came from an old man sitting behind him. Elie listened carefully, for he quickly understood that his informant had a message for him that he disguised while appearing to be fervently praying.

Elie had already learned that one major fear of Russian Jews was right within their midst. They feared that among them were people who betrayed them to the authorities. Spies among their own. Jews themselves, these informers mingled at airports, synagogues, Jewish meetings, and reported everything they heard to the government.

Elie never turned around to see the old man behind him. He did not wish to cause him trouble, but he was very grateful to him for his ingenuity in revealing information. It was thus that Elie learned how difficult Jewish life was in Kiev, how the teaching of Torah was outlawed, that anti-Semitism was widespread. Worst of all, the old man mourned that the Jewish spirit was deteriorating under so much pressure.

When he returned to Moscow in time for Simhat Torah, the Rejoicing of the Law, Elie, as a guest of honor in the synagogue, carried the Torah in the customary procession around the sanctuary. After the service a major surprise awaited him. In the square outside Moscow's main synagogue a crowd of at least 30,000 young people were gathered, singing and dancing Jewish songs in honor of the holiday. It was a spontaneous celebration; no one had planned it. Tears ran down Elie's cheeks as he heard them sing *Am Yisroel Hai*—"The Jewish People Lives."

Elie noticed a beautiful, sparkling young girl who seemed to be leading the joyful demonstration. He was able to squeeze through the crowd and press her hand. Having so recently learned how difficult it was to be Jewish in the Societ Union, he asked the girl why she chose to remain Jewish. "Because," she answered, "to be Jewish is to sing."

Between the ardent desire of Russian young people to remain Jewish and the sadness of older Jews over the repression of their religion ran a common cry. It said, "Help us." The cry was not lost on Elie. For many months after he left the Soviet Union it pursued him. His book *The Jews of Silence* was published in 1966. It was the first time that attention had been drawn to the plight of Russian Jewry and it unleashed a major worldwide effort on their behalf.

Elie carried another memory out of Russia with him. He had attended a Kol Nidre service during which he was much moved by the old rabbi's utter hopelessness and despair. Elie could not forget him. He kept wondering what the old man would really say if he had been free to express himself. In his imagination Elie created a literary character much like that rabbi who exploded in rage at the official repression of religion. In his play, *Zalmen, or the Madness of God*, the unforgettable old man lets go of all his fears and becomes a spokesman for all the persecuted, frightened victims of the godless, totalitarian society Russia had become.

Elie's book and his play stimulated interest in the plight of Soviet Jews. In time this interest was believed to have opened gates that led to Soviet Jewish emigration. Years later Elie stated in an interview that he thought it a miracle. "If anyone had told me that one day we'd see the Russian Jews emigrating in such numbers, I would have thought they were crazy. Nobody would believe it could happen in my time."

From the very birth of their state, Israelis had expected that one day the strong feelings of their neighbors, fueled by the constant agitation of the

Soviet Union, would boil over against them once more. The seething anger over Arab defeats in 1948 and 1956 had never cooled down completely. Since then, leaders of the Arab states had been moving full speed toward another war. Israel knew it was only a matter of time before she was attacked again.

On June 5, 1967 the whole world awoke to the news that Egypt had attacked Israel by air and land. Within hours Elie carried a slim suitcase and his travel typewriter aboard an El Al flight to Tel Aviv. By now he was a correspondent well known in both the American and Israeli press, and it was important for him to cover this breaking story, both professionally and emotionally. But even he was surprised at the stream of travelers who disembarked at Ben-Gurion airport from the fully-loaded planes arriving from all parts of the globe. Israel was at war, yet instead of leaving, people—Jews and non-Jews—were arriving in droves to help.

Since its birth the State of Israel had given new pride and moral support to Jews everywhere. It was an important emotional fortress and the one home where all Jews are welcome. If Israel were to fall to the guns of her threatening neighbors, Jews in the outside world would stand isolated. A second annihilation of fellow Jews during one lifetime was unthinkable. It was a very real threat. As Elie was to write, "The shadow of Auschwitz finally enveloped Jerusalem."

But the shadow paled quickly. Within five days the war was over: Egypt was driven back into the desert,

Syria gave up the Golan Heights, the Jordanians retreated. For the first time in nineteen years Jerusalem was united again.

The sight of victorious Israeli soldiers kissing the stones of the Wall in the Old City made a tremendous impression on Elie. Israel's sons had given their blood and their lives to prevent another Holocaust. So deeply imbedded did this scene become that he made it the backdrop of one of his most important books, *Beggar in Jerusalem*. The main theme running through various subplots of *Beggar* mirrors a conviction close to its author's heart. Judaism survives. It is eternal despite the efforts by its enemies throughout the ages to destroy it.

13

One
Generation
After

Elie has always kept his personal life very private. He spent many long years alone, feeling that the events of his youth had left him with ghosts from which he needed to free himself before he could think of getting married and having a family. He needed to find his balance before he could commit himself to such a big step. And, as he frequently says with a smile, he had to wait for the "right person" to come along.

His friends rejoiced when in the late 1960s Elie met Marion Erster through mutual acquaintances in New York. She seemed to be the "right person" for whom he had been searching. On Passover Eve 1969, just as springtime spread renewed warmth and hope over Israel, Marion and Elie stood together on the *bimah* of

Jerusalem's ancient Rambam Synagogue and exchanged wedding vows in a small, very private ceremony conducted by Professor Saul Lieberman, Elie's Talmud teacher and close friend.

Marion, a blonde with lustrous dark eyes, is a strongly-motivated, charming, and highly intelligent woman. Vienna-born, she is also a camp survivor and shares Elie's sense of purpose. She is a marvelous linguist and since their marriage has become his literary

Elie and his wife, Marion.
(Photograph by William Coupon)

partner, translating most of Elie's books from French into English.

Getting married was Elie's most affirmative personal step. He had waited a long time to undertake it. For someone so acutely aware of symbols, being married in Israel in springtime meant a great deal to Elie. Those who knew him well hoped that his marriage would mark a new beginning in his life.

In 1970 Elie's tenth book, *One Generation After,* a collection of stories, was published. With it Elie stopped writing about the Holocaust. He had always suspected that it would take him at least ten books to give his testimony. Twenty-five years had gone by since his liberation from Buchenwald. He had become so strongly associated with the Holocaust that many people tended to think of him exclusively as a permanent witness.

He has written more than thirty books and two plays since *Night.* None of them deal directly with the Event, but all were written because of it. Elie, the writer, felt it was time to write about other topics. "The teller of tales has turned the page," he stated.

June 6, 1972 was a day of special joy and profound spiritual meaning for Elie and Marion. It was the day their son was born.

Elie was forty-four years old when he became a father. He was awed by the responsibility of bringing a child into a world that he felt was not a good place for children. "When he was born, I felt very sorry for him," Elie told a reporter. "I felt sorry for him coming into this ugly, difficult, horrible world. Now I still feel sympathy, but naturally the urge is much stronger than before to try to do what we can to make it a little better. Because he is here, we try."

Even greater than his sense of responsibility was his feeling of happiness at knowing that his family would continue. The baby was named Elisha (Shlomo ben Eliezer). Elie carried his son to the circumcision

Elie and his son, Elisha, studying Talmud.
(Photograph by William Coupon)

ceremony, which was held in the living room of their Central Park West apartment. He was overwhelmed at the touching words of the officiating hasidic rabbi, "A name has returned." At the ceremony tears filled Elie's eyes at the thought that some day, at his Bar Mitzvah, the boy would be called up to the Torah with the same name Elie's father once bore when, as a Bar Mitzvah, he stood before the Holy Ark in Sighet. It represented a strong link to the past and to an ancient tradition. To Elie it confirmed once again that, despite all attempts by force to cut it, that link has survived unbroken.

Over the years Elie has lectured around the world. When he returns to France he experiences a special nostalgia whenever he is invited to lecture at the Sorbonne. Once in his own early days as a penniless, stateless refugee student he, too, sat in these same seats, in this same hall, struggling to understand the French language, battling the gnawing demons of his immediate past.

Now Elie stands at the speaker's podium lighted by a small light and looks out at the many rows of seats in the huge darkened auditorium. Faced by a sea of student faces he is overcome by strong feelings. It seems incredible that he should stand here now and be paid to speak in French to a new generation of French students about his favorite topic, the hasidic masters whom he loves so dearly. Inevitably he thinks of a quotation that is especially meaningful to him:

God sees, God watches. He is in every life, in every thing. The world hinges on His will. It is He who decides how many times the leaf will turn in the dust before the wind blows it away.

The Baal Shem Tov, saintly founder of Hasidism, spoke these words to his disciples so long ago. When he repeats them, Elie thinks of the Carpathian Mountains where they were first uttered. He also thinks of Sighet and his own childhood, and of Dodye Feig from whom he learned them.

In Manhattan, where for many years Elie's Thursday night lectures at the 92nd Street YMHA have always been sold out, his audiences contain many familiar faces. Since his first "Y" lecture on Job in 1976, this subscription series has become so popular that people travel to hear it from as far away as Pennsylvania and Massachusetts. Some of the "regulars" return year after year.

In the total silence of the hall Elie's soft-spoken words transport his listeners back to a long-gone world. The tales and legends he recites belong to a time when pious people believed strongly that prayer and faith in God could produce miracles in their hard daily lives.The legends tell of struggles to overcome sadness and fear with faith and joy. For the impoverished Hasidim, so threatened by assaults from the outside world, this was not an easy task. Yet their Masters tried to defeat despair by believing in God, love, and the eventual coming of the Messiah and taught their followers to believe just as strongly.

Fascinated since his childhood with stories about

the hasidic masters, especially with the life of the Baal Shem Tov, Elie tells his audiences that the Baal Shem never allowed his students to write down anything about him. Everything he taught had to be transmitted orally from one generation to the next. As these stories moved through time, no one knew for certain what the original teaching had been, or how much had been added on during the transmission. Thus they became legends.

Fact or fiction, the followers of the Baal Shem believed the legends because they wanted to or needed to. Therefore the message was never lost: there is a living relationship between God and His people. Elie quotes the Baal Shem:

> He told them what they wanted to hear: that every one of them existed in God's memory, that every one of them played a part in his people's destiny, each in his own way and according to his means.

In passing on the age-old message, Elie too, sustains and enriches those who come to hear him.

Using the notes of his Paris and New York lectures, Elie wrote the book he always wanted to write. *Souls on Fire,* the first of his works on the lives of the hasidic masters, was published in 1972.

Teaching has always been a beloved and major part of Elie's life. He began teaching university students at New York's City College in 1970 with a course on the Holocaust. When he first taught the course he sensed that many of his students were themselves children of survivors who needed to find a way to understand the fears and reactions of their parents. It demands the greatest sensitivity on his part—and theirs—to face the past with his students. Sometimes both he and his students are left drained by readings that plumb the depths of hatred and evil.

For the last eighteen years Elie has taught at Boston University, where he is Andrew Mellon Professor in

Elie lecturing a class of students at Boston University. (Boston University Photo Service)

the Humanities. His seminars and classes have waiting lists of students eager to take a course with Professor Wiesel. Before being admitted to his class, a student must be interviewed and granted permission to attend. When he faces his students, he leaves his hectic world of public appearances, flight schedules, or television interviews outside the classroom. With his wispy hair tousled, his shirt collar opened, and his tie loosened, he cups his head in his left hand and fully concentrates on his students as together they study some of the world's great literature. This work means much to him. It reminds him of the small *shtiebel* of his youth, where the followers of the Tzaddik surrounded their teacher and drank in his every word. Only now it is he, Reb Eliezer, who is the teacher.

He loves young people. Both his teaching and his writings are aimed at them. Students return his affection for a very important reason: Elie tells them that it is wrong to despair. He teaches them to affirm life, to live each day to the fullest, and, most importantly, to remain human. He is the best example of his teachings. His own life has become a lesson in how to overcome incredible obstacles and emerge as a triumphant human being.

In his mid-sixties he still rises before six A.M., sleeps very little, and writes from six to ten in the morning. He spends every free minute studying Talmud and the books of the Bible. He enjoys life as only a survivor can, knowing how very precious time is and how important it is to make the most of every moment. "My life is full. The main thing is not to waste time," he says.

Humanity and staying human is of the utmost interest to Elie. He believes the Jewish people has survived primarily because it has always responded to suffering by remaining human. He likes to say that by all rights the Jewish people should have disappeared from the world a long time ago. There has never been a period in history where Jews were not persecuted, sometimes—as in our age—almost to the point of extinction. What has saved them, while other civilizations have died out, is their human response.

14

Memory May Be Our Only Answer

In November 1978 President Jimmy Carter invited Elie to become the first chairman of the President's Commission on the Holocaust. It was an honor Elie welcomed. The Commission's purpose was his goal, too: the need to remember. This was a mission close to his heart.

The President's Commission became the United States Holocaust Memorial Council. For the next seven years Elie traveled from New York to Washington regularly, guided innumerable meetings, and pondered with other committee members how best to remember the victims of hate in a permanent, meaningful way. Eventually the Memorial Council agreed on a museum or study center. If people learned that government action and public apathy could lead to murder, the warning might prevent such a future happening.

The Memorial Council also inaugurated another commemoration. On April 24, 1979 Elie stood in the Capitol Rotunda in Washington, D.C. and addressed a gathering which included President Jimmy Carter, the Congress, and hundreds of guests. On this, the first Day of Remembrance, the crowd listened in silence to the haggard man whose dark eyes held such deep sadness. With a soft weary voice Elie recalled the day during Passover Week exactly thirty-five years ago when a young Jewish boy, his family, and ten thousand other Jewish occupants of his small home-town were rounded up and sent into exile and death.

Elie spoke of arriving in camp, of seeing the flames that devoured little children, and he remembered that he had asked his father how this nightmare could be happening in the midst of the civilized twentieth century. His father had replied, "Perhaps the world does not know."

"The world knew and kept silent," Elie's breaking voice assured his deeply-moved audience.

Elie thanked the President for remembering. "No other country and its government, besides Israel, has issued or heeded such a call."

The Hebrew words of the Kaddish echoed throughout the Rotunda of the United States Capitol and long tapers in a menorah were lighted. Elie said, "Memory may perhaps be our only answer, our only hope to save the world from ultimate punishment, a nuclear holocaust."

In Elie's mind the echoes of the Holocaust resound in places and times far removed from the actual event. They touch generations still unborn. And he is profoundly sad whenever he learns of new hatreds and killings throughout the world. He has written and spoken out against episodes of hatred and violence in Biafra, Lebanon, Northern Ireland, Vietnam, Central America, South Africa, and Israel. "Hate is like cancer," he has said. "Once it has started it is too late."

He continues to remember that no one protested the forced departure of the Jews of Sighet. The image of the indifference of a whole town has never left his memory. That image still prods him to write, speak, and teach that indifference is an even greater sin than hate. And that those who see evil and do nothing are just as guilty as those who commit the evil deed.

"After the war, I thought I could change the world by telling the story," Elie has said. "This is the Jewish belief: that out of total darkness will come total light."

In February 1980 Elie, deeply troubled by the suffering of the Cambodian people in their struggle against a cruel dictatorship guilty of murdering millions in its "killing fields," joined an international March of Survival to bring food and medication across the border from Thailand into Cambodia to survivors of the killing who were plagued by disease and hunger. For him it was not difficult to remember how it had felt to be hungry, alone, and forgotten. He was painfully aware that once again the eyes of the world were turned the other way.

A group of 150 people, among them celebrities from many countries, was organized by the International Rescue Committee and the French "Doctors Across Frontiers." The group had brought twenty truckloads of supplies for distribution among the victims of oppression, war, and famine.

On a hot, dusty day the marchers faced hostile border guards in a tiny Thai border town called Aranyaprathet. The guards would not let them or their precious supplies enter Cambodia. No amount of negotiation and pleading succeeded. The marchers turned back and sat down in the parched dirt of the bridge between the two countries, and held a vigil.

For Elie this day marked a special anniversary. On this day thirty-five years ago he had lost his father in Buchenwald. The pain of the loss and the awareness of its circumstances had never left him. Whenever he thought of his father he remembered that Shlomo always tried to help people. It seemed extraordinarily appropriate to Elie that he should be in this place on this day. "I came here because nobody came when I was *there*," he said.

He found nine more Jews among the group. In their company Elie stood on the dusty Thai bridge and recited the Kaddish for his father.

The work of the U.S. Holocaust Memorial Council bore fruit when in October 1980 the President of the United States signed a bill passed by both houses of Congress, which authorized the building of a permanent Holocaust museum/memorial in the city of

Washington, D.C. The law also called for the dedication of specific Holocaust Days of Remembrance to be held each year on the anniversary of the Warsaw Ghetto uprising.

As honorary chairman of the World Gathering of Jewish Holocaust Survivors, Elie saw another dream come true in June 1981. As a youngster in the concentration camp, Elie, along with many others, entertained the fervent hope that one day everyone who had shared and survived that experience might meet again. Such a meeting would honor those who had died. Perhaps it would just demonstrate that there were survivors, testifying to the failure of the Nazis to exterminate every Jew they had planned to kill.

Almost seven thousand participants came to Jerusalem for the reunion. They came from every part of the world and brought their wives, husbands, and children. For three days and nights thousands of survivors crowded the streets and open air plazas. A few even found family members or friends long believed lost, recited a highly emotional Kaddish led by the chief cantor of Israel's armed forces, and sang *Hatikvah* with heartfelt fervor. The survivors pledged that the Holocaust was an event which "must never be forgotten, never be repeated."

A second gathering in Washington, D.C. followed two years later, attended by many thousands who had not made it to the Jerusalem gathering.

Elie in front of the White House in Washington, D.C. with his wife and son. (Courtesy of Elie Wiesel and Elirion, Inc.)

15

The Anatomy of Hate

In recognition of his life's work as a novelist, playwright, speaker, and witness to the Holocaust, Elie received the Congressional Gold Medal of Achievement from the hands of President Ronald Reagan on April 19, 1985, at the White House in Washington, D.C. It was a singular honor and a moment of enormous pride for Elie. In his acceptance speech Elie thanked the American people for honoring him, and with him the survivors of the Holocaust who had found a new life in the United States. He expressed his appreciation for the great humanitarian spirit of the U.S. Congress and for its help in establishing and sustaining the State of Israel.

President Reagan was scheduled to depart shortly afterward on a diplomatic trip to Germany. One of his planned activities there was a visit to a military cemetery where a number of officers of the Waffen SS were buried. The very name "Waffen SS" recalled to Elie the picture of the death's head insignia on the black uniforms and steel helmets of the hated German soldiers who had patrolled the streets of Sighet and had instilled such fear in its inhabitants. Elie thanked President Reagan for his friendship toward the Jewish people, and for his continuing efforts to free Soviet Jews. But then, with great pain in his voice, he expressed dismay at the proposed presidential trip to Bitburg cemetery. Citing the Talmudic tradition that requires one to "speak truth to power," Elie begged President Reagan not to go there. "That place, Mr. President, is not your place. Your place is with the victims of the SS."

It took great courage for Elie, a courteous, polite man, to speak so frankly to the President of the United States. His statement, made at a ceremony honoring him, could easily have been interpreted as arrogant or insulting to President Reagan. But Elie was prompted by great moral reasons. To him it was unthinkable that an American leader should pay his respects to an enemy responsible for so much evil. Statecraft or not, to Elie it was was primarily a question of right or wrong.

Afterward both the U.S. Senate and the House of Representatives held debates and offered resolutions urging the President to change his plans. Neither they nor the highly publicized "Bitburg Speech" had the desired effect. President Reagan followed the prompting of his German host, Chancellor Helmut Kohl, ignored the protests of survivor and veteran groups, and visited the military cemetery in Germany.

In October 1985 Elie returned to Washington for the groundbreaking ceremony of the U.S. Holocaust Memorial Museum on the Mall near the Washington Monument. The building which had been decided on and planned during his period of leadership would soon rise here, and Elie hoped it would be both a momument of remembrance and an inspiration to prevent future genocides. He was pleased that his committe had reached this point despite many obstacles and political opposition.

Not long afterward Elie resigned his chairmanship of the U.S. Holocaust Memorial Council. In his letter of resignation he cited one of his reasons: "Bitburg has left a bitter taste." He continued his demanding schedule of teaching and writing, and traveling worldwide to keep his lecture commitments.

The ringing of the telephone at five o'clock in the morning on October 15, 1986 awoke Elie and Marion in their Manhattan apartment. It was the day after Yom Kippur and Elie was still groggy from the daylong fasting and praying of the highest Jewish holy day.

"Mr. Wiesel, I am Jacob Sverdrup of the Nobel Institute in Oslo and I want to tell you that you have been selected to be the recipient of the 1986 Nobel Peace Prize. Congratulations, sir."

Elie was overwhelmed. He remembered that late on the previous afternoon on the way home from the synagogue a reporter had approached him. Speaking with a heavy Norwegian accent, the man had told him his Oslo newspaper was planning a front-page story for the following day announcing Elie Wiesel as the next Nobel Peace Prize winner. Smiling, Elie had told the reporter to make sure the news was not a mistake. Now he knew it had not been a mistake.

From Norway came the words of the Nobel Committee, calling him a spiritual leader in an age of violence and hatred and praising "Wiesel's commitment, which originated in the sufferings of the Jewish people, and has been widened to embrace all repressed peoples and races." The president of the Norwegian parliament, who had been one of several Scandinavian legislators to nominate Elie Wiesel, said, "Never has his message—the fight against growing terrorism and contempt for human beings—been more timely."

Later in the day Elie held a news conference in the crowded auditorium of the 92nd Street YMHA. He said, "I decided to devote my life to telling the story because I felt having survived I owe something to the dead. That was their obsession, to be remembered, and anyone who does not remember betrays them again." The award and the $270,000 in prize money would allow him "to speak louder" and "reach more people" in his attempt to promote the causes he has pursued throughout his adult life.

When a reporter asked whether receiving the Nobel Prize would change him, Elie replied, "If the war did not change me, you think anything else will change me?"

*Elie, Marion, and Elisha in New York on the day
Elie was announced as recipient of the Nobel Peace
Prize. (Courtesy of Elie Wiesel and Elirion, Inc.)*

Less than two months later, in Oslo, Norway on December 10, 1986, fourteen-year-old Elisha stood beside his father on the podium of Oslo University's ceremonial hall. He had been invited there by the Nobel Committee in a symbolic gesture to show that despite the Holocaust the chain of generations had not been broken. For a brief moment Elie's hand rested on his son's shoulder. With tears in his eyes Elie asked the permission of Norway's King Olaf V to cover his head in the presence of royalty. Then he placed a yarmulke on his head before chanting the Hebrew blessing, "Blessed is the Lord our God, Ruler of the universe, for giving us life, for sustaining us and for enabling us to reach this season."

The ceremony lasted one hour. In absolute silence the invited audience listened as Elie was praised for his work in the years since he was liberated from the concentration camps. The mood was one of memory. Everyone was touched by it. Elie felt it strongly. "I sense their presence," he said softly. "I always do— and at this moment more than ever. The presence of my parents, that of my little sister ..."

His acceptance speech contained both a description of his personal mission and a warning for the future. "This honor belongs to all the survivors, to their children and, through us, to the Jewish people with whose destiny I have always identified," he said. "We must always take sides. Neutrality helps the oppressor, never the victim. Silence encourages the tormentor, never the tormented.... Whenever men or women are persecuted because of their race, religion, or political views, that place must, at that moment, become the center of the universe....

"I have tried to fight those who would forget. Because if we forget, we are guilty, we are accomplices. If we forget, then they will be killed a second time."

Later he thanked the Nobel Committee and the people of Norway for showing through the award that the survival of the Jews "has meaning for mankind." The audience applauded him as he held up the gold Nobel medal and the accompanying certificate inscribed with the citation, "Elie Wiesel is a messenger to mankind. His message is one of peace and atonement and human dignity. The message is in the form of a testimony, repeated and deepened through the works of a great author."

Then, surrounded by Marion, his son, and friends, Elie left the hall and walked out into the growing darkness of the Norwegian afternoon.

With part of the funds from the Nobel Peace Prize, Elie established the non-profit Elie Wiesel Foundation for Humanity. It is the embodiment of his desire to seek and find answers. For a very long time he had hoped to bring together a group of people who, like him, wanted to make the world aware of the major problems that make the twentieth century a time of violence and hate. He selected talented, knowledgeable members to search out urgent topics, and at three annual meetings to report on how they might be resolved.

What would happen if the combined brain power of

the world's most creative minds were harnessed for a distinctly useful purpose? At the presidential palace in Paris in 1988 Elie's idea became reality. The French government joined the Elie Wiesel Foundation for Humanity in co-sponsoring a four-day conference of seventy-five living Nobel laureates from eighteen countries. The topics of the conference were indicative of present world concerns: nuclear disarmament, hunger, AIDS, human rights. President François Mitterand, Elie's long-time friend, welcomed the illustrious assembly and urged it to "discuss the intractable problems of a century producing barbarism in the midst of progress."

Elie, who had organized the spectacular gathering of world figures, was very conscious that its opening day fell on the anniversary of an event that had great meaning for him. It was forty-three years earlier to the day that the Nazis had abandoned Auschwitz. Only the day before Elie appeared at the Paris conference of Nobel laureates, he had visited the grounds of the death camp where he lost his mother and little sister, Tsiporah. He had embraced another Nobel laureate, Lech Walesa of Poland, in an emotional meeting before a monument dedicated to camp victims. Now, in Paris, he hoped that he and his colleagues could start a new period of education and awareness, one that would be "asking for all human beings the right not to suffer."

16

The Prophecy Fulfilled

In early spring of 1993 Elie visited Bosnia-Herzegovina, part of former Yugoslavia but now a country torn apart by internal violence. Ancient feuds between peoples who lived within the same borders had erupted into ethnic fighting between Serbs and Muslims and could not be quelled by any outside peacekeepers. There were rumors of concentration camps, atrocities, murder, and rape. Anyone who tried to enter the country to help risked being killed. United Nations forces tried to deliver food and medical aid to Muslim victims, but most supplies were waylaid by Serbian forces and did not reach their intended recipients.

And so Elie entered the dangerous war zone to, as he says, "bear witness." He came there as he had long ago gone to the Jews of the Soviet Union, to the Cambodian border in search of victims of the "killing fields," to South Africa to see for himself the effects of apartheid, to Argentina where he sat with the mothers of the *desaparecidos* (the "disappeared"), and to Hiroshima where he commemorated the victims of the atomic bomb with a wreath at a memorial to the dead. Again, the important reason for his trip was that no one had come while he was in the Kingdom of Night.

Television anchormen flew on the plane with him and interviewed him enroute to Bosnia. Camera crews followed him and recorded his every reaction on the streets of once-proud Sarajevo, now a city under constant siege of gunfire. His photograph, in which he looked small, sad, and bereft in battle helmet and flak jacket, appeared in newspapers worldwide.

In Bosnia he indeed found several locations where people were kept in concentration camps under barbaric conditions unhappily reminiscent of his own experiences. He spoke to inmates who would surely be punished for their revelations once Elie had left, but who spoke anyway. He was under constant mortar fire from Serbian forces who demoralized the civilian population by their never-ending attacks, killing men, women, and children indiscriminately.

Elie spoke to the leaders of both sides. He begged for an end to the "ethnic cleansing," the horrid term used by the Serbs to cover their murder of non-Serbian people. Government leaders gave him promises he knew would never be kept: promises to observe a cease-fire, promises to let supplies through, promises to stop the fighting permanently. It was a trip that left Elie tremendously discouraged and depressed. He knew that neither side of the conflict had been completely honest with him. Not even the voice of a Peace Prize laureate had been sufficiently forceful to persuade political leaders to stop the killing.

Shortly after Elie's return from Bosnia the U.S. Holocaust Memorial Museum was officially opened. The opening occurred on April 22, 1993, during the week that coincided with the Warsaw Ghetto uprising exactly fifty years earlier. It was a miserably cold and rainy day in Washington and the mood of the eight thousand guests, Holocaust survivors and world leaders, who huddled under umbrellas during the outdoor ceremony, matched the somber weather. Located near the Washington Monument and overlooking the Jefferson and Lincoln Memorials on its west, the architecture of the new stark-looking building is in strong contrast to them. The U.S. Holocaust Memorial Museum brings to mind both visually and emotionally some the darkest deeds in human history.

On a dais set up in front of the building were written the words of Elie Wiesel, "For the dead and the living, we *must* bear witness." These words have become the motto of the Holocaust Museum. At the speaker's podium beneath his words, Elie once again explained the need to remember, "To forget would mean to kill the victims a second time. We could not prevent their first death; we must not allow them to be killed again."

In an anguished voice he mentioned his sleepless nights since his recent return from Bosnia. The unspeakable horror he had seen there had convinced him that the interference of outside nations was absolutely necessary to bring about a cease-fire and a permanent peace. "We cannot tolerate the excruciating sights of this old new war," he said. Turning to President Bill Clinton, he implored, "Mr. President, this bloodshed must be stopped. It willl not stop unless we stop it."

Receiving the Nobel Peace Prize has added enormous responsibility to Elie's life and increased its already rapid tempo. The urgency to help people, inherited from his father, now covers whole countries. He confers with heads of state, religious leaders, and political representatives, when he can influence moral decisions in government or give his advice on humanitarian causes.

Although the Nobel Peace Prize laureate Elie Wiesel has now reached the high point of fame and is described as a modern prophet, a great writer, and a brilliant teacher, deep within himself Elie still sees himself as "a *yeshivah bucher* from Sighet." To him the Nobel award was a new beginning. With it have come new responsibilities and new obligations, and the need to work even harder than before to warn others of the dangers of apathy and complacency.

He still believes that he was saved from the Nazi Holocaust for a purpose.

He is deeply saddened and shocked at the new wave of racial and ethnic intolerance boiling up all over the world.

He is furious at the "revisionist" scholars, both in Europe and in the United States, who publish books claiming the Holocaust never took place; at the "skinheads" who beat up foreigners and torch their homes; at the merciless massacres that destroy whole segments of populations because they are minorities or "different."

And, once again, he is saddened by the world's silence as new faces in windows all over the globe watch and do nothing.

In Elie's book-lined study on an upper floor of a high-rise apartment on Manhattan's East Side, a recording of classical music plays softly. Elie is working at his desk, writing out by hand the main thoughts of a speech soon to be delivered during one of his lecture commitments. He likes to have the sounds of chamber or choir music in the background when he writes. It soothes him.

He still observes the rigorous routine of rising early to write or study from six to ten in the morning. Sometimes he works at two or three books at once. When he writes he manages to build a "wall of silence." He becomes totally oblivious to whatever goes on around him. It is a gift to be so completely absorbed: he can interrupt his work in mid-sentence, hold a telephone conversation, then return to finish his thought or sentence.

Elie in his book-lined study.
(Photograph by William Coupon)

At the present time he has published thirty-five books, several plays, innumerable speeches. The purpose of his writing and his teaching is the same as it has always been: "Memory can be the only way to save the future ... by maintaining the past."

"Everything I do, I do as a Jew first," he says proudly. His happiest moments are those he manages to spend with friends who, like him, share a hasidic background. He still loves to sing hasidic melodies that remind him of his grandfather, Dodye Feig. On special occasions he dances hasidic dances in a group where he is not a celebrity but an equal in a tight circle of friends. The study of Jewish texts is a daily necessity for him. It keeps him refreshed and guides his life in a proper perspective.

To a man who believes there are no accidents in life, only encounters that are meant to happen, a curious episode occurred not too long ago. A distant cousin who also lived in New York asked Elie, "Do you remember the last time you and your mother visited the Wishnitzer Rebbe, when your mother cried for weeks afterward?" Certainly Elie remembered.

Sarah Wiesel had spoken to that cousin later during that long-ago day. And now, so many years later, Elie finally received the Wishnitzer Rebbe's mysterious answer, which his mother had never revealed to him.

When Sarah had asked the Rebbe about Elie's future, this had been his answer: "Sarah, daughter of David, I want you to know that one day your son will grow up to be a great man in Israel, but neither you nor I will be alive to see it."

Over Elie's computer hangs a framed black-and-white photograph, the picture of a small wooden house, the home of the Wiesel family in Sighet. His eyes stray to that picture frequently. But he does not need reminders. The memory of the past has never left him.

GLOSSARY

aleph, bet, gimel
First three letters of the Hebrew alphabet.

Baal Shem
Israel ben Eliezer, known as the Baal Shem Tov ("Master of the Good Name"), or "Besht," for short. Founder of the hasidic movement in Poland in the 1750s.

Bar Mitzvah
Literally: "son of the commandments" (fem. Bat Mitzvah: "daughter of the commandments"). Person who becomes duty bound to observe the commandments of Judaism on reaching the age of thirteen (twelve or thirteen for a girl). Also refers to the ceremony celebrating this "coming of age."

bimah
Elevated platform containing the reading desk from which the Torah is read in a synagogue.

bistro
Small restaurant or wine shop.

B'nai B'rith
Literally: "Sons of the Covenant." Oldest and largest
Jewish service organization, founded in 1843 in New York.

caftan
Ankle-length garment of cotton or silk with long sleeves
and sash fastening, usually worn by hasidic men.

cheder
Traditional Hebrew school for young children.

chometz
Leavened bread removed from the home during the week
of Passover, when only unleavened bread *(matzah)* is
allowed.

crematoria
Furnaces used by the Nazis for burning human bodies.

El Al
National airline of the State of Israel.

Final Solution
Term used by Nazis in describing the destruction of
European Jews.

ghetto
Restricted area in a city where Jews were forced to live.

Hasid
Literally: "pious one." One who practices the beliefs of a
Jewish religious movement founded in Poland in the
1750s.

Hasidim
Plural of "Hasid."

Hatikva
Literally:" The Hope." The national anthem of the State
of Israel.

Ivrit
The Hebrew language.

Juden-rein
German term meaning "free of Jews."

Kabbalah
Hebrew term meaning "tradition," usually referring to the Jewish mystical tradition. It can also refer more broadly to teachings transmitted orally from generation to generation.

Kaddish
Hebrew for "Sanctification," a prayer recited by mourners.

kapo
A veteran concentration camp prisoner in charge of policing newcomers.

knaidel
Term for "dumpling," used primarily in describing matzah balls eaten during Passover.

knaidlach
Plural of "knaidel."

kugel
A delicious casserole or soufflé-type dish served as an accompaniment to meats or as a dessert.

Kol Nidre
Opening prayer recited at synagogue services on the evening of Yom Kippur. Also refers to the entire evening service.

kvittlach
Yiddish term describing small pieces of paper containing questions or requests to be used in interview with a rebbe.

Maariv Service
Hebrew name for evening service.

maggid
Itinerant preacher or storyteller who uses biblical material as basis for his lectures.

melamed
Hebrew word for "teacher." Usually applied to traditional Hebrew teacher of small children.

Messiah
"Anointed." A divinely chosen descendant of King David who will in the End of Days bring redemption or salvation to the Jewish people and the entire human race.

mitzvah
Good deed. (Literally: "commandment")

oral tradition
Body of Jewish laws and traditions not contained in the Torah and not written down, but transmitted from generation to generation by rabbinic interpretation or folkways.

OSE
Oeuvre de Sécours aux Enfants. French social work organization.

Passover
Seven-day holiday (eight days among Orthodox and Conservative Jews outside of Israel) commemorating the Exodus from Egypt.

payes
Earlocks worn by hasidic males.

Pirke Avot
Ethics of the Fathers, a tractate of the Mishnah.

Rosh Hashanah
Jewish New Year. Begins the first day of the Ten Days of Penitence.

seder
A festival meal held on the first two nights of Passover (one night in Israel and among Reform and Reconstructionist Jews).

Shabbat
Hebrew: "Sabbath," the seventh day of the week, Saturday, set aside for rest, study, and prayer.

Shavuot
Feast of Weeks, time when God gave the Ten Commandments on Mt. Sinai.

Simhat Torah
Festival of "Rejoicing in the Law," occurring at the end of Sukkot.

shtiebel
Small room used for Jewish communal prayer or study.

Talmud
Authoritative body of Jewish tradition comprising the Mishnah and Gemara.

tefillin
Two black leather cubes with long leather straps containing biblical passages on parchment, worn on the forehead and arm during daily morning prayers, except on Shabbat and holidays, by Jewish males age thirteen and older.

Torah
The Five Books of Moses. Sometimes refers to Jewish learning in general.

Zohar
The fundamental work of Jewish mysticism.

IMPORTANT DATES
in the life of Elie Wiesel

1928 September 30 Eliezer Wiesel, the son of Shlomo and Sarah Wiesel, is born on Simhat Torah in Sighet, Transylvania.

1931 Elie is enrolled in *cheder* at age of three and is taught by a succession of Hebrew teachers.

1935 Little sister Tsiporah is born.

1937 Elie and his mother visit the Rebbe of Wishnitz for the last time.

1939 Germany invades Poland. Killing of Jews begins there.

1940 Transylvania becomes a part of Hungary, a partner in the Germany-Italy-Japan "Axis."

1941 Elie asks his father to find him a Master to teach him the Kabbalah. Moshe, the synagogue caretaker, becomes his teacher.

1941 Hungary enters the war in June by joining Germany in attacking Russia. Hungarian Jews lose their citizenship. First deportation of "stateless" Jews begins, among them Moshe, the synagogue care taker, Elie's Master.

1942 Elie becomes a Bar Mitzvah.

1944 *March 19.* Germany occupies all of Hungary. Nazi soldiers start patrolling the streets of Sighet. At dawn of last day of Passover Jewish community leaders are arrested in Sighet. Everyone else is put under three days of house arrest. Every Jew must wear a large Star of David sewn on his or her clothing for identification. A ghetto is established where Jews live behind barbed-wire fences, separated from the Christian population.

Beginning in May the Jewish population of Sighet and of all Hungary is rounded up, placed in cattle cars and deported to Nazi concentration camps.

Arriving in Auschwitz, Elie and his father are separated from his mother and sisters. Sarah and little Tsiporah are killed almost immediately. Elie becomes prisoner #A-7713. Shlomo and Elie spend the summer, fall, and winter in Auschwitz, Buna, and Buchenwald concentration camps.

1945 *January 29.* Shlomo dies at Buchenwald.

April 11. American armed forces liberate Buchenwald. Elie and several hundred other children from the camps are brought to France, where relief organizations help them to recuperate from their ordeal. Elie takes vow of silence regarding his family's experiences.

1946 At age eighteen a stateless, impoverished Elie begins life in a Paris rooming house. Enrolls as a student at the Sorbonne, the University of Paris.

1948 Birth of State of Israel. Elie becomes Paris correspondent for Israeli newspaper *Yedioth Ahronot.*

1949 Elie travels to Israel for the first time.

1952 Elie travels throughout the world.

1953 Interviews French writer François Mauriac, who urges him to break the vow of silence.

1954 Elie writes eight hundred page Yiddish version of his memoirs, *And the World Stayed Silent,* printed in Argentina, but rejected in France.

1955 Elie cuts and rewrites his manuscript in French, entitled *La Nuit* (Night). Mauriac helps him get it published in France.

1956 Elie comes to New York City as United Nations correspondent for *Yedioth Ahronot.* Works as editor for *Daily Jewish Forward.* Is hit by a taxicab in Times Square and disabled for many months.

1959 *La Nuit* is published in France and receives rave reviews.

1960 *Night* is published in the United States. Elie becomes an American citizen. Covers Jerusalem trial of Adolf Eichmann as a reporter.

1961 The novel *Dawn* is published.

1962 Elie travels to Germany for the first time. The novel *The Accident* is published.

1964 Elie returns to Sighet on first visit since being deported. The novel *The Town Beyond the Wall* is published. Elie receives the literary Prix Rivarol in France, the National Jewish Book Council Award in the United States, first of many honors for his writings.

1965 During the Jewish High Holy Days, Elie travels to the Soviet Union for the first time. Trip results in writing of *The Jews of Silence.*

1966 Receives B'nai B'rith Jewish Heritage Award for Literary Excellence. Begins speaking career.

1969   Is married to Marion Erster in Jerusalem ceremony on Passover Eve.

1970   *A Beggar in Jerusalem* is published. *One Generation After*, his tenth and last book dealing directly with the Holocaust, is published. Begins teaching Holocaust courses at City College, New York.

1972   *June 6.* Elie and Marion's son, Elisha, is born.

1976   Elie begins his Thursday night lecture series at Manhattan's 92nd Street YMHA. Becomes Andrew Mellon Professor of Religion at Boston University.

1978   President Jimmy Carter appoints Elie to head the President's Commission on the Holocaust. The Commission becomes the U.S. Holocaust Memorial Council and eventually recommends the establishment of a museum/study center.

1979   *April 24.* The first annual national Day of Remembrance takes place at the U.S. Capitol.

1980   Elie joins marchers attempting to bring food and medical supplies across the border from Thailand into Cambodia to aid victims of Cambodian genocide.

1981   *June.* First World Gathering of Jewish Holocaust Survivors takes place in Jerusalem.

1985   *April 19.* Elie receives U.S. Congressional Gold Medal of Achievement from President Ronald Reagan. During White House ceremony Elie makes "Bitburg Speech."

   October. Groundbreaking for U.S. Holocaust Memorial Museum takes place. Shortly afterward Elie resigns his chairmanship of the U.S. Holocaust Memorial Council.

1986 *December 10.* Elie receives the Nobel Peace Prize in Oslo, Norway. Uses some of his prize money to start the Elie Wiesel Foundation for Humanity.

1988 The French government and the Elie Wiesel Foundation for Humanity cosponsor a Paris conference of seventy-five Nobel laureates to discuss world problems and possible solutions.

1992 Elie receives the Medal of Freedom from President George Bush in a White House ceremony.

1993 Elie visits war-torn Bosnia "to bear witness."

April 22. Is main speaker at the opening of the U.S. Holocaust Memorial Museum in Washington, D.C.

BIBLIOGRAPHY

Abramowitz, Yosef L.
"Is Elie Wiesel Happy?" Broward (Fla.) Jewish Journal,
February 3-9, 1994.

Berger, Joseph.
"Witness To Evil: Eliezer Wiesel." *New York Times,*
October 15, 1986.

Erem, Gabriel and Jeannette Friedman.
"A Noble Man of Conscience—Always Searching for
Answers." *Lifestyles,* Fall 1992.

Markham, James M.
"Elie Wiesel Gets Nobel for Peace As 'Messenger.'"
New York Times, October 15, 1986.

Schemo, Diana Jean.
"Holocaust Museum Hailed as Sacred Debt to Dead."
New York Times, April 22, 1993.

Stern, Ellen Norman.
Elie Wiesel: Witness for Life. New York: KTAV Publishing
House, 1982.

Works by Elie Wiesel

Night, a memoir. New York: Hill and Wang, 1960.

Dawn, a novel. New York: Hill and Wang, 1961.

The Accident, a novel. New York, Hill and Wang, 1962.

The Town Beyond the Wall, a novel.
New York: Avon Books, 1964.

The Gates of the Forest, a novel. New York:
Holt, Rinehart, and Winston, 1966.

The Jews of Silence, a personal testimony. New York:
Holt, Rinehart, and Winston, 1966.

Legends of Our Time, essays and stories. New York: Holt,
Rinehart and Winston, 1968.

A Beggar in Jerusalem, a novel. New York:
Random House, 1970.

One Generation After, essays and stories. New York:
Random House, 1970.

*Souls on Fire: Portraits and Legends of the Hasidic
Masters*. New York: Random House, 1972.

The Oath, a novel. New York: Random House, 1973.

Ani Maamin, A Song Lost and Found Again, a cantata.
New York: Random House, 1973.

Zalmen, or the Madness of God, a play. New York:
Random House, 1974.

*Messengers of God: Portraits and Legends of Biblical
Heroes*. New York: Random House, 1976.

Four Hasidic Masters, more portraits and legends. Notre
Dame, Ind.: University of Notre Dame Press, 1978.

A Jew Today, essays, stories, and dialogues. New York:
Random House, 1978.

The Trial of God, a play. New York: Random House, 1979.

The Testament, a novel. New York: Summit Books, 1980.

Images from the Bible. The Words of Elie Wiesel, the
Paintings of Shalom of Safed. Woodstock, N.Y.:
Overlook Press, 1980.

Five Biblical Portraits. Notre Dame, Ind.: University of
Notre Dame Press, 1981.

Somewhere a Master, more Hasidic tales. New York:
Summit Books, 1982.

Paroles d'étranger, essays, stories, and dialogues. Paris: Editions du Seuil, 1982.

The Golem, the retelling of a legend. New York: Summit Books, 1983.

The Fifth Son, a novel. New York: Summit Books, 1985.

Signes d'Exode, essays, stories, and dialogues. Paris: Editions Bernard Grasset, 1985.

Against Silence: The Voice and Vision of Elie Wiesel, collected shorter writings edited by Irving Abrahamson. 3 volumes. New York: Holocaust Library, 1985.

Job ou Dieu dans le Temps d'été, dialogue and commentary with Josey Eisenberg.
Paris: Editions Fayard-Verdier, 1986.

A Song for Hope, a cantata. New York: 92nd Street Y Publication, 1987.

The Nobel Address: Hope, Despair and Memory. copyright Nobel Foundation, 1986; special printing of 3,000 copies, Summit Books and Boston University.

Twilight, a novel. New York: Summit Books, 1988.

The Six Days of Destruction, with Albert Friedlander. Mahwah, N.J.: Paulist Press, 1988.

Silences et mémoire d'hommes, essays.
Paris: Editions Grasset, 1989.

From the Kingdom of Memory, reminiscences.
New York: Summit Books, 1990.

Evil and Exile, dialogues with Philippe-Michel de Saint-Cheron. Notre Dame, Ind.: University of Notre Dame Press, 1990.

A Journey of Faith, with John Cardinal O'Connor.
New York: Donald I. Fine, 1989.

Sages and Dreamers, Portraits and Legends from the Bible, the Talmud and the Hasidic Tradition.
New York: Summit Books, 1991.

Célébration talmudique, Portraits of Talmudic Masters, Paris: Editions du Seuil, 1991.

The Forgotten, a novel. New York: Summit Books, 1992.

A Passover Haggadah, with commentary by Elie Wiesel, illustrations by Mark Podwal. New York:
Simon and Schuster, 1993.

INDEX

Note: page numbers in italics indicate photographs